DESTROY CARTHAGE!

Books by Alan Lloyd

ANTIQUITY
Destroy Carthage!
The Taras Report
Marathon

GENERAL HISTORY
The Spanish Centuries
(España a Traves de los Siglos)
The Year of the Conqueror
(American title: The Making of the King 1066)

BIOGRAPHY
King John
(American title: The Maligned Monarch)
The Wickedest Age
(American title: The King Who Lost America)
Franco

MILITARY HISTORY
The Scorching of Washington
The Drums of Kumasi
The War in the Trenches
The Hundred Years War
The Zulu War

NOVELS
The Eighteenth Concubine

DESTROY CARTHAGE!

The Death Throes of an Ancient Culture

by
ALAN LLOYD

SOUVENIR PRESS

Contents

CONTENTS

BOOK ONE

A*

MAPS

following 4 pages

THE MEDITERRANEAN OF CARTHAGINEAN TIMES

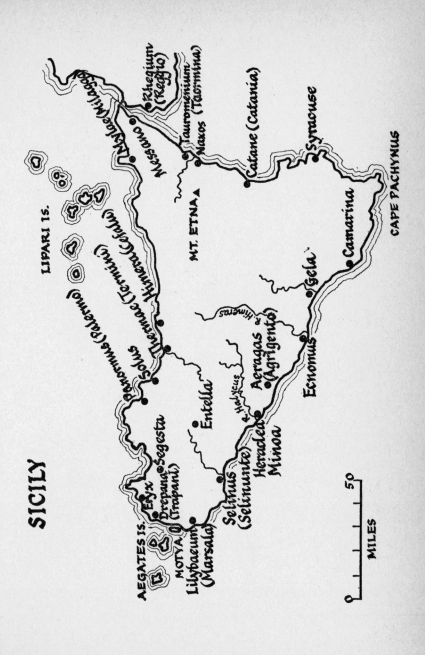

SICILY

LIPARI IS.

AEGATES IS.
Eryx
MOTYA
Lilybaeum (Marsala)
Drepana Segesta (Trapani)
Entella
Selinus (Selinunte)
Heraclea
Minoa
Halycus
Panormus (Palermo)
Solus
Thermae (Termini)
Himera (Imera) (Cefalù)
Mylae (Milazzo)
Messana
Orontes
Rhegium (Reggio)
Tauromenium (Taormina)
Naxos
Catane (Catania)
MT. ETNA
Himeras
Agragas (Agrigento)
Gela
Ecnomus
Camarina
Syracuse
CAPE PACHYNUS

0   50
MILES

CARTHAGE HARBOUR COMPLEX

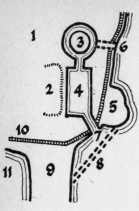

1 Byrsa
2 Tophet
3 Naval harbour
4 Merchant harbour
5 Choma or outer quay
6 Emergency channel cut during siege
7 Regular harbour entrance
8 Mole built by Romans
9 Taenia
10 City wall
11 Lake of Tunis

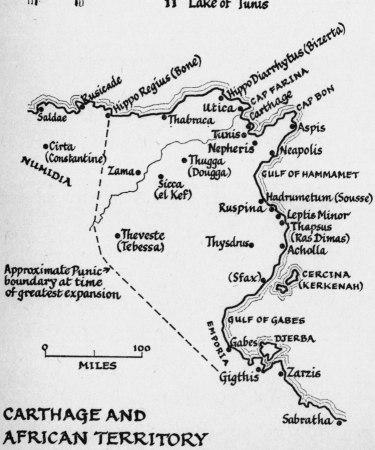

Approximate Punic
boundary at time
of greatest expansion

MILES   100

CARTHAGE AND
AFRICAN TERRITORY

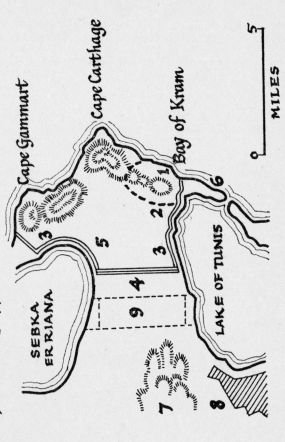

CARTHAGE showing approximate position of defenses

1 Harbours and Tophet 2 Inner walls of Byrsa 3 Coast walls 4 Triple defenses across isthmus 5 Megara 6 Taenia 7 Hill of Arriana 8 Modern Tunis 9 Roman blockade during final siege.

1: *The Numidian*

SURVEYING the Bay of Carthage from the modern *Plage d'Annibal*, it is difficult to believe that here, in its age, stood the greatest merchant centre of the western world; that from the sands of that tawny, inert shore sailors sought mysterious Thulsa in the northern mists, traders braved the Sahara for Pigmy gold, generals marched turreted elephants to distant wars.

Few cities of such stature have disappeared so profoundly, more violently. The relics are minimal. This is the story of that disappearance, of the extinction at a stroke of a civilized, thriving state; the history that lingers on a haunted coast. Among the ghosts to be discovered as the tale unfolds, not the least assertive may be the first.

Two centuries before Christ, the plateau of Maktar, in present-day Tunisia, was the territory of Masinissa, king of the Numidians. To the writers of antiquity, Masinissa was a barbarian, a cunning savage with a varnish of culture acquired from neighbouring Carthage and the Romans. His prurience, an alleged distinction of the Numidians, was catalogued. He was said to have fathered forty-one sons among his progeny, the last in the eighty-seventh year of a prodigious life.

Masinissa's ambition matched his procreative energies. In his youth, Numidia comprised two kingdoms, the Massylian to the east, with a royal town at Zama – identified with Jama, north of Maktar – and a western realm based on Cirta, now Constantine. Masinissa coveted Cirta from an early age. Scarcely beyond boyhood, the precocious prince led his followers, sanguinary horsemen who rode their barbary ponies bareback, into western Numidia, first driving its ruler, Syphax, to seek refuge with the Moors; somewhat later, seizing his capital and his wife.

At the same time, Masinissa flirted dangerously with Mediterranean power politics. The skill and ferocity of his mounted warriors gave his friendship a value to greater states. In the stormy relationship between Rome and Carthage, he switched alliances according to the run of luck, fighting for one then the other with equal zest. Each wooed him, yet, with justification, distrusted him. Dismayed by his passion for Sophonisba, the nubile Carthaginian wife he took from Syphax, the Romans induced him to engineer her suicide. For the major powers, confrontation was a grim game with heavy costs. For Masinissa, it meant profit, the fulfilling of his appetites.

His kingdom prospered wonderfully. Its treasury multiplied, its army grew, it even obtained a fleet. Despite turbulent chieftains, whom he checked with a heavy hand, Masinissa increasingly turned his eyes to distant parts. His envoys made overtures in Egypt and Libya. Perhaps his dreams were pan-African. Certainly, his subjects, once a plundering tribe of the meseta, became an organized and flourishing people: a force, some feared, which might unite the entire north of the subcontinent.

As the 3rd century BC – a century of desperate violence in the western Mediterranean – approached its conclusion, Masinissa was in his prime. Below his native plateau, on the gulf of Tunis, a hundred miles or so from Zama, lay Carthage, the templed queen of Africa, her lands and associates established on the coastal plain. Masinissa envied her markets, her busy harbours, her influence and knowledge.

Beyond the city, across the sea Carthaginian traders had once called their own, republican Rome, still shaken by Hannibal's aggression, stubbornly reaffirmed her role of expansion in world affairs: a role Masinissa was ready to utilize. These were the fulcrums of his strategy; the first, rich in the resourcefulness and enterprise of her Phoenician heritage, a gem worth all the stones in Numidia; the second, a steely tool which might yet chip the prize from bedrock into its neighbour's lap.

To the east, Greece and Egypt continued their long decline, secondary on Masinissa's skyline, while westward, Spain, the uncivilized object of colonial rivalry, marked the end of the ancient world – at least for all save a tiny band of daring men. It was from the settlements in Spain that the latest clash of the great powers, the Second Punic War of history, had spread to Italy and, now in its final throes, swayed to Africa.

Two years before the new century, the dust of advancing armies accented the Numidian marches. A Roman column was moving from the coast up the valley of the river Bagrades (Medjerda), penetrating the elevated hinterland behind Carthage. At its head rode the brilliant Publius Cornelius Scipio, distinguished later as 'Africanus Major.' His father and uncle had died in Spain campaigning against the Carthaginians. Scipio, succeeding to their command, had been conspicuous in wresting the initiative from Hannibal.

Simultaneously, Hannibal himself, returned from Italy, advanced to intercept the foe. The battle which followed their conjunction near Zama was preceded by a celebrated interview. Bringing the rival generals face to face for the first time, the meeting captured the imagination of the ancient world. 'Mutual admiration struck them dumb,' exclaimed Livy. 'They gazed at each other in silence.'

Hannibal Barca, reflected in numismatic portraiture as craggily handsome with a curly mane, already a byword for audacity, was willing to make peace. Hope of winning the war with Rome had faded, but an awesome reputation supported the proposition he essayed. A Roman defeat now would blemish his rival's fame. Better an amicable compromise, he declared, than to gamble for more on the battlefield.

Scipio, whose thin-lipped, shaven-headed effigy suggests a practical and penetrating intellect, was a move ahead. Numerically, the armies were balanced, though Hannibal alone possessed elephants, the heavy assault vehicles of the age. Scipio's confidence reposed in a pact with Masinissa whereby the king's mounted warriors would provide the Romans with cavalry ascendancy.

Unfortunately, Masinissa had been occupied chastising a factious chief, and was late arriving with his horsemen. Ostensibly disposed to negotiate, Scipio was more concerned to kill time than reach a settlement. Masinissa's approach assured the failure of the interview. The battle of Zama was fought next day.

It was autumn in the year 202 B.C.

Scipio deployed his legions in three lines, the companies dressed by the front with passages between them from van to rear. As Hannibal's elephants, eighty-strong, lumbered forward, many passed harmlessly into the corridors, to be harried by missile-hurling skirmishers. Others, inadequately trained for warfare, ran amok at the blare of battle. Prepared for the contingency with lethal bolts to drive into the heads of their ungainly mounts, the handlers found it hard to effect instant execution. Threshing and squealing, the maddened animals stampeded into Hannibal's cavalry which, disordered, was pursued from the field by Masinissa's horse.

The contest devolved on infantry. With neither side abundant in seasoned troops, Hannibal was handicapped additionally by the heterogeneity of his force. The Carthaginian army – matching the enemy at about 40,000 men – comprised a mixed bag of Africans, Ligurians, Gauls, Macedonians, Balearic Islanders and others, the majority mercenaries. Apart from some veterans brought back from Italy, they were unaccustomed to campaigning together, prone to factional distrust.

Hannibal chose to hold his seasoned men in reserve. His front line, following the elephants, contained Gauls, Ligurians, Balearians and Moors. They attacked boldly, but Scipio had closed his companies behind the tuskers, and the enemy recoiled, mauled, from a solid wall of legionaries. There was momentary confusion as the Carthaginian lines coalesced. The second comprised levies from the city and its territories. Angered by the repulse of the mercenaries, the home troops drove them roughly to either flank.

At this juncture, Hannibal and Scipio brought their units into single line. With the cavalry absent in flight and pursuit, the opposing infantry surged together across ground slippery with blood to form an attenuated mass of struggling warriors.

The conflict was desperate. Then Masinissa reappeared.

Having abandoned the mounted chase, the Numidian wheeled his foam-flecked cavalcade round the battling host and, accompanied by Scipio's cavalry captain, Laelius, charged Hannibal's infantry in the rear. It was the decisive stroke. Shocked and divided, the Carthaginian force disengaged and fled leaving heavy losses on the battlefield. Roman victory was complete.

As Scipio advanced on an apprehensive Carthage, he was forestalled by a deputation of citizens bearing olive branches and ready to receive his terms. His immediate requirements were soldierly. All Roman deserters and prisoners were to be handed over; all war elephants to be surrendered; all naval vessels given up except for ten galleys. Scipio demanded money and grain for the Roman troops.

Then came the indemnity. Carthage was held liable for a sum of ten thousand talents of silver payable by instalments over fifty years. For a city of vast resilience and wealth-accruing capability, it was hard but not ruinous. Worse were the territorial clauses. On the one hand, Carthage was to surrender all lands which had ever belonged to Masinissa and his ancestors, nomadic tribes whose wanderings raised issues of dispute.

On the other hand, she was forbidden to make war, even in Africa, without Roman consent. Whether this precluded resort to arms in defence of her own boundaries was ambiguous, but it certainly ruled out retributive or pre-emptive movements across them. Thus, plainly exposed to contentious claims, Carthage no longer had the right of direct redress. With such despair did some regard these terms that there was talk of continued resistance.

A certain Gisco, arguing this course in the senate at Carthage, was manhandled by those who saw the uselessness of further fighting. For a contrary reason, Rome lacked unanimity over the treaty. The consul, then Cnaeus Lentulus, opposed a settlement, loath to let Scipio get all the glory. If the war continued, at least in formality, Lentulus might himself gain credit for delivering the *coup de grace*, or exacting even tougher terms.

But the Roman people were for Scipio. Lentulus was over-ruled by popular vote and it was proposed to make the victorious general not only consul but dictator of Rome for life – honours he declined, to resume before long his foreign services. So, in the spring of 201, after seventeen years of constant fighting, Rome and Carthage forswore hostility and looked to new relationships.

Masinissa was not done. Virtually invited to make free with Carthaginian territory, he surveyed the frontiers of his neighbour with mounting cupidity. True, Carthage could turn to Rome for arbitration in land disputes, but Rome, as the wily king realized, had no favours to return her old enemy.

2: *City Bearings*

THE historian Appian described Carthage as a ship at anchor off the coast of North Africa. More accurately, the configuration was that of a thick wedge driven east into the gulf of Tunis, its point at Cape Carthage, its leading faces culminating at Cape Gammarth to the north, to the south at the bay of Kram. From Kram to Gammarth is seven or eight miles.

Connecting the head of the wedge to the continent, a neck of land varying from two-and-a-half to three-and-a-half miles in width passed between what was then a northern gulf of the sea – now the Ariana lagoon, or Sebka er Riana – and the southern lake of Tunis, the ancient Stagnum Marinum. While the neck was of low ground, the broader head of the promontory contained a series of heights, contributing to the illusion noted by Appian.

Three areas of high land may briefly be identified.

In the south, an elevated region marked the site of the old quarter of the city, the Byrsa or acropolis, its seaward declivity dropping to the bay of Kram and the harbour complex. In the central region, an agglomeration of hills, rising inshore of Cape Carthage, terminated to the south in the now St Louis hill, where the Byrsa began, and to the north near the present village of Sidi Bou Said. Beyond the latter extremity, running to Cape Gammarth, was the so-called Catacomb hill (Djebel Kawi).

Distinct from the Byrsa, or city proper, the ancients identified the Megara, the greater area of Carthage, its suburbs and semi-rural aspects stretching inland of the hills toward the throat of the isthmus, where the civil boundary was defined. Westward, straddling the plain behind the promontory, a further range of heights concealed the distant hinterland.

The population of the city in the years after Zama has been

estimated at 200,000, thinly spread in the Megara, teeming in the markets and docklands. Here, the economic heart of Carthage, with its whitewashed façades, its jumble of tenements and terraced dwellings, its flat roofs and vaulted roofs, its twisting alleys and steep streets climbing to the Byrsa, probably presented many similarities to those towns of the eastern Mediterranean which survived until recent times – still survive, in some places – with few concessions to modern change.

Those familiar with North Africa will readily imagine the out-of-door display of produce and artefacts, the craftsmen huddled at cluttered portals amid solemn infants and sleeping dogs. In the heat of day, parts of the city, rudimentary in sanitation, were far from fragrant. But the evenings, redolent of night-scented flora and the warm, nocturnal breezes of the continent, must have conjured longing in absent Carthaginians.

Like their Phoenician ancestors, the city's architects were capable of building massive and durable structures, as the defences will demonstrate. Dwelling apartments in three streets descending from the Byrsa toward the docks rose, in some cases, to six storeys. Generally, however, the low cost of labour and the availability of cheap, light materials, discouraged monumental work.

Friable limestone from deep quarries on Cap Bon, across the gulf, was used for important buildings, and in the foundations of others. But most houses were of unbaked brick and puddled clay, faced with stucco. The outer walls, it seems, were largely blank, domestic life concentrating on inner courtyards where cool floors might be found of a characteristic pink cement mixed with marble chips.

Since Carthage has left no writing of her own, and archaeological evidence is limited, the best attested features of the city are those which evoked the most wonder among ancient chroniclers. The shrines, numerous and profoundly revered by the populace, were famed throughout the civilized world of the period. Some were austere, mere areas of bare ground devoted to the powers believed to dwell or appear there.

This type of holy place, the *tophet* of Hebrew terminology, was represented near the Byrsa by the sanctuary of Tanit, fore-most spirit of the Carthaginian pantheon. Occupying an area of valuable dockland running the entire length of the merchant harbour, it contained the burnt bones of thousands of children sacrificed to the deity down the centuries of the city's life. Less forbidding were the temples, rich in statues and gold and silver offerings. Of these, the most renowned was that of Eshmoun, the god of vital force and healing. A flight of sixty steps approached its precinct from the Byrsa.

Not far from the temple, was the north end of the harbour complex. The Carthaginians had built their harbours, probably by the elaborate transformation of natural pools, on the low-lying alluvial shore beside the Byrsa plateau, seemingly in a situation still occupied by two lagoons at Salammbô. The commercial harbour, connected by a southerly channel to the bay of Kram, was rectangular in plan, about 1,600 by 1,000 feet, between the sea and the sanctuary of Tanit.

Here came merchantmen from all shores of the trading world: Italy, Greece, the Levant, Egypt and elsewhere. Many foreign businesses had permanent agencies in Carthage, and parts of the city housed communities of alien merchants. Down the years, their presence had enriched the culture of the great port. Essentially, Carthage had grown rich on commodity brokerage, traditionally importing raw materials, especially metals, from the west and exporting them east, or to the Africans of the interior.

The Carthaginians were not manufacturers of special note, but as entrepreneurs and sailors they excelled. Their naval skills were outstanding. The military harbour, circular and perhaps 1,000 feet in diameter, was attained through the merchant basin, at the north end of which was a linking channel. According to a description based on the evidence of the historian Polybius, who examined the complex:

The harbours were arranged in such a way that ships could pass from one to the other, while the entrance from the sea, 70 feet wide, could be sealed by iron chains. The first harbour, devoted to merchant vessels, contained numerous berths. In the centre of the inner (naval) harbour was an island which, like the circumference of the basin, was lined with quays, the entire waterfront being given to boat-houses with accommodation for 220 ships.

Each boat-house was flanked by two Ionic columns, so that the front of the harbour and of the islands resembled a sweeping portico. On the island stood the admiral's head-quarters, also used by the trumpeters and heralds. Since the island rose steeply from the water, the admiral could observe what was happening outside, but little could be seen of the basin from the sea beyond. Even from the merchant harbour the arsenals remained concealed, for they were surrounded by a double wall.

Strabo, writing later, added that the channel between the harbours, as well as the pools themselves, was banked by covered berths. This extraordinary complex, diverging from the normal use of natural harbours, echoed a traditional Phoenician preference for man-made ports. The classic sources describe it as a *cothon*. Though small in water area, it could accommodate substantial fleets, for the ships were not moored but kept ashore in the boat-houses.

At Carthage, the obvious defensive advantages of such an arrangement were enhanced by a massive stone structure, including a parapet, which screened the entrance of the *cothon* from the gulf, ranging north for some distance seaward of the merchant basin. Known as the *choma*, this appears to have served a dual purpose in protecting the outer channel from rough weather and amphibious attack. It may also have been used as a quay by ships of call not wishing to enter port.

Not the least fantastic of the works at Carthage were the mighty outer ramparts of the city. Inspiring grandiloquent portrayal by ancient writers, despondency in hostile generals, the walls were about twenty-three miles in length, longer than the celebrated walls of old Syracuse.

The vital section of the fortification – that straddling the isthmus to repulse attack from the mainland – was more than fifty feet high, and almost thirty feet thick at the base, with four-storey towers every seventy yards or so. Within this wall was a double tier of remarkable casemates, the lower providing housing for 300 elephants; the upper, stables for 4,000 horses. The rampart also contained barracks for the cavalrymen, the elephant handlers and 20,000 infantrymen, together with storage for arms and provisions.

In front of this extraordinary obstacle was another rampart, of now unknown character. Ahead again lay a moat sixty feet wide backed by a palisade of earth, stone and timbers. Faced with this triple barricade across the neck of the promontory, few enemies even contemplated a land attack. Assault from the sea was given little better chance, for, apart from the power of the Carthaginian navy at most times, a modified but formidable extension of the wall followed the entirety of the coastline round the greater city.

There was also a wall, reputedly of some two miles, round the Byrsa, forming an inner citadel above and inland of the docks, overlooking the senate house and main public square. In all, it was a daunting system. Thus had the greatest commercial city in the Mediterranean, some said the richest in the world, protected her people, her businesses and sanctuaries – and, in her best times, the huge stocks of gold that tantalized rival states.

Before those walls, Agathocles the Greek and his general Eumarcus had recoiled; the mercenaries of Matho and Spendius had stopped short. After Zama, there had been officers who urged Scipio to reduce Carthage. Scipio's philosophy demanded the dependence, not the destruction, of Rome's enemies, and his African army had toiled enough. Had he been of another mind, the ramparts must have prompted second thoughts.

3: *The Exile*

A curious detail of the treaty of 201 was that Rome did not insist on the indictment of Hannibal, her greatest enemy. It is known that he supported the peace after Zama against those in Carthage who talked of further resistance. It may be that Scipio was moved by the freemasonry of generals. It was also a fact that the Carthaginians were notorious for dealing harshly with their failed commanders, and Rome may have left them to their own judgement.

If so, she regretted it. Far from being traduced, Hannibal retained sufficient support in Carthage to discourage political opponents from seeking his arraignment. Until 196, he lived discreetly in retirement, then, disgusted by increasing corruption in government, returned to public life.

The immediate problems of the city on the morrow of defeat were concerned with morale and the financial burdens of the treaty. These were not helped by an administration of conniving nobles which, while raising taxes, arranged the exemption of its own members and embezzled the revenues. Popular resentment, expressed in the election of Hannibal as sufet, chief magistrate, led to swift reforms.

When the board of judges, a self-perpetuating clique of aristocrats appointed for life, obstructed him, Hannibal won enthusiastic backing for the annual review of its membership. He went on to show that by eliminating tax avoidance and other public scandals, the indemnity to Rome could be met without the need for extra taxes. His support grew.

Within a few years of his supposed vitiation, the general Rome had feared more than any other man on earth was reestablished as a force to be reckoned in a recuperative and increasingly democratic Carthage. Neither the Roman senate nor the Carthaginian politicians discredited by Hannibal liked the developments. Insidiously, a story was spread linking the 'warmonger' with the eastern emperor Antiochus of Syria in a plot against the Latin state.

In 195, three Roman agents arrived in Carthage, ostensibly on diplomatic business but in fact to deal with Hannibal. Suspecting that the purpose of the visit was his erasure, and that powerful local interests might assist in it, the former general fled secretly to Thapsus, on the gulf of Hammamet, where he shipped for the Levant with a private fortune. To placate the frustrated Romans, his political enemies destroyed his house and property.

Syria, on the other hand, welcomed the exile as an honoured friend. Whatever his earlier relationship with its ruler, Hannibal had now been driven to the eastern camp. At Antioch, he learned that the emperor was in the far west of Asia Minor, at Ephesus, contemplating the shores of Greece. The Seleucid dynast had extensive plans.

Three years before Zama, the accession of a child Pharoah to the pristine throne of the Nile had prompted Antiochus to make a compact with his fellow-imperialist, Philip V of Macedon, whereby they would divide the external dominions of Egypt between their lands. Fearfully, the Egyptians had looked to Rome for protection while, equally alarmed, a number of smaller eastern realms pledged alliance with the western power.

At peace with Carthage, the Romans switched their efforts to the new zone, in 200 declaring war on Macedon. Macedonian troops, they recalled, had fought for Hannibal at Zama. Further, Roman prospects in the Balkans were threatened by Philip V.

The venture, a notable one in Rome's history, for it marked a significant shift from concern with her own safety toward the making of her greater empire, started slowly. Scipio was preoccupied with domestic tasks. It was not until 197, when a young consul named Titus Flaminius took command, that fortune swung dramatically. Flaminius, deflecting the Greek states from alliance with Macedon by offering himself as their liberator from Philip's yoke, then smashed the Macedonians at Cynoscephalae, in Thessaly.

Commencing in thick fog, and fought over hilly ground, the battle proved a triumph for the tactical flexibility of the Roman legions against the less adaptable phalanx traditional to the Balkan states. Philip, his army decimated, was obliged to surrender his fleet and abandon his Greek possessions.

In a masterly appearance at the Isthmian games, Corinth, the victorious Flaminius now proclaimed the Greek nations independent, free not only from Macedon but of obligation to Rome herself. The announcement, received with delight by the Hellenes, shrewdly disposed of any leanings they might have toward the Syrian empire, ensuring the continuance of a number of weak bodies rather than a powerful bloc. *Divide et impera* was already a Roman theme.

Meanwhile, Antiochus, too busy enriching himself to assist his co-conspirator, had seized Cyprus and several Egyptian lands in Asia Minor. He also exploited Philip's predicament to annex the Dardanelles and parts of Thrace. Well on his way to recreating the old Seleucid empire, he had superseded Carthage as Rome's outstanding enemy when Hannibal fled east.

At Ephesus, the Carthaginian propounded his own strategy. Rome could only be vanquished in Italy if large numbers of her troops were tied up abroad. In Spain, the turbulent tribes once encountered by Carthage were keeping a strong Roman force occupied. If another were obliged to defend Greece against Syrian invasion, a simultaneous seaborne attack on Italy might succeed. Hannibal offered to lead a Syrian armada to Italian shores.

It was a bold scheme; perhaps the last chance to dispute the mastery of the world before Rome became unchallengeable. But Antiochus, lacking Hannibal's western insight, temporized. With much to lose, the Asian monarch preferred to move cautiously. Rome took the initiative. In 193, a courier from Hannibal was arrested in Carthage and the Romans, apprised of the eastern debate, sent agents to Ephesus to investigate.

By this time Scipio had resumed foreign duties and may have accompanied the mission. Livy and Plutarch, recounting a second interview between the generals, framed a well-known anecdote. Scipio was supposed to have asked the Carthaginian to name the greatest commanders in history, to which Hannibal responded with Alexander, Pyrrhus and himself, in that order. 'Suppose you had beaten me?' inquired Scipio ironically. 'Then I would have been the greatest of all,' replied Hannibal.

More convincing is the information that the attention accorded Hannibal by the Roman agents disturbed Antiochus, who henceforward demoted the exile in his councils. War was now inevitable. In 191, both Rome and Syria landed expeditions in Greece, Antiochus apprehensively retaining the bulk of his forces at Ephesus. The indecisive army he advanced was demolished by the Romans at Thermopylae.

Command of the Aegean became crucial. If the Romans were not to move east onto his preserves, Antiochus needed every ship he could muster on that sea. Accordingly, Hannibal returned to Tyre to fetch reinforcements, but they never joined the king's fleet. Sailing north, they were worsted in the bay of Adalia by the warships of Rome's ally, Rhodes. Hannibal withdrew with the surviving craft of the beaten force. When Antiochus's Aegean squadrons were defeated at Myonessus, the water no longer protected him.

The invasion he feared came in 190, jointly led by Scipio and his brother Lucius. Antiochus, falling back from Ephesus to the river Hermus (Gediz Chai), stood to fight at Magnesia, modern Minissa, his army computed at 74,000 warriors. The Scipios led two Roman legions and proportionate allied contingents, perhaps 30,000 troops. Since Publius had taken ill and could not leave his sick-bed, Lucius engaged the enemy. The Romans affected disdain for them, a view with which Hannibal now concurred.

According to Cicero, he described a military lecture at Ephesus as the dissertation of an old fool. Asked his opinion of Antiochus's army, Hannibal is said to have observed: 'It will be sufficient – however greedy the Romans may be.'

Certainly, Antiochus had displayed little confidence in with-drawing so far before a much smaller force, but Hannibal had not despised the king's troops before Thermopylae, and Magnesia showed that they could yet be dangerous. For a time, the Romans were in jeopardy. While their ranks drove at the enemy's centre and left flank, Antiochus himself led his right wing in an advance that compelled part of the Roman army to withdraw to its battle camp. Only the steadfastness of a courageous tribune circumvented disaster, allowing time for reinforcements to come up.

Thwarted on the verge of success, Antiochus departed. His army, leaderless and demoralized, soon followed. Theirs was a long retreat, for the terms eventually agreed confined the Syrians beyond the Taurus range, leaving Rome to exploit Asia Minor.

The arrest of Hannibal again appeared imminent. Believing that Antiochus might betray him to the Romans, the Carthaginian embarked for Crete. There, the treasure he still carried disturbed his peace. Distrusting the motives of his hosts, who knew of his private wealth, he turned back to Asia, seeking refuge in the hilly northwestern district of Bithynia, then feuding with its neighbour and rival, Pergamum.

Apparently the Bithynians had Hannibal to thank for a form of biological warfare they used against the ships of their enemy. Pots were filled with snakes and hurled at the hostile craft. As the missiles smashed, venomous reptiles swarmed among the terrified sailors of Pergamum.

Ingenious ruses proliferate in the literature of Hannibal's later years, adversity repeatedly foiled by an agile mind. Now the fugitive immobilizes a suspicious flotilla by persuading its captains to use their sails as weather shelters. Now he sets a false trail for those who seek his treasure, topping clay-filled jars with a skin of gold. Factual or apocryphal, the tales express the constant dangers of the exile's life.

Rome dogged his travels unforgivingly. When negotiations with Bithynia revealed his whereabouts to the Latin senate, extradition once more threatened. This time, there was no escape. In his sixty-fifth year, Hannibal was too old a bird, as Plutarch put it, to fly again. Rather than submit to capture, he killed himself by drinking poison – to relieve 'the great anxiety of the Romans,' he apostrophized.

The year was 183. Fate had already tagged a companion for his sombre shade. Within twelve months, Publius Scipio was dying at Liternum, Campania, as disillusioned and embittered as his old foe.

4: *The Censor*

THE circumstances of Scipio's death introduce a new and ominous participant to the drama of Carthage. He first appears – a sedulous soldier-politician as conscientious in criticism as in his duties – with the general at Zama. Then thirty-two, of hardy Tusculum farming stock, Marcus Porcius Cato had risen by stubborn will and ability to a rank of note in Rome, recently holding office as quaestor, or paymaster.

Soon he would be aedile, praetor and consul in quick succession, later becoming censor, by which title he is best known.

According to Livy, Romans of a future generation regarded Cato as the personification of old school manners, of severe, inflexible attitudes already thought reactionary by many in his lifetime. His ethos was stern in its simplicity. He despised luxury and extravagance, attacking their manifestations with relentless impartiality. He railed tirelessly against relaxed morals, especially among the young, and in women, whom he seems to have viewed with misogynistic rancour.

Respected widely as embodying traditional Roman traits, Marcus Cato cannot be recalled as an endearing man. Privately, he was a hard husband, seemingly regarding his wife as a household slave; an unaffectionate father; an often cruel master to his servants.

In office, he was diligent, repairing aqueducts, supervising the cleansing of sewers, ensuring the safety of public places, generally scourging what he saw as social mischief. Since he disapproved implacably of the new ideas concomitant with Rome's expanding experience in the 3rd and 2nd centuries, this was a sweeping brief. Among other things, he resisted the fashionable importation of Hellenic culture and urged the expulsion from Rome of foreign philosophers. The popularity of alien religious cults disgusted him.

Zama found Cato serving under a soldier of very different character. Scipio, though essentially a man of action, was broad-minded, cultured and magnanimous – a strange mixture of patriot and cosmopolite, mystic and adventurer. Convinced of Rome's imperial and protective mission, he applied himself to martial and diplomatic tasks with a worldliness far removed from the rigidities of Cato.

Long, dangerous campaigns, often far from reinforcement, had taught Scipio the value of rewarding his troops in victory and of showing restraint to beaten enemies. Meanness commanded the devotion neither of the Roman soldier nor his allies, and very real devotion had been Scipio's through a decade of campaigning up to Zama. In Africa, as elsewhere, he indulged both his men and himself generously in their triumphs, distributing spoil open-handedly.

Cato's austere sensibilities were duly shocked. The future censor did not conceal his disapproval of such wasteful extravagance. By the time the Hannibalic war ended, the political opponents of Scipio had gained an officious and outspoken friend.

In the opening years of the new century, Cato was prominent not only in administration but as a force for colonial repression. After holding a command in Sardinia, he acquired a cruel reputation in 194 subduing the resistance of Spanish tribes. Three years later he landed in Greece as a tribune under consul Manilius Glabro to oppose the Syrian invasion. As vigorous in battle as in the senate, Cato distinguished himself at Thermopylae by leading a column through the hills to take the enemy in the rear.

Back in Rome, his stature now formidable, Cato became the animating spirit of a series of attacks against Scipio and his brother Lucius for their handling of the Syrian War in its final phase. The generous foreign policy of Scipio, the easy terms he proposed for Antiochus, his approval of Greek culture – all became ammunition for the doughty Cato in a feud which had assumed bitter proportions since Zama.

Honourably, if rashly, Scipio managed his defence in a singularly unprofessional fashion – on ground dominated by the enemy, and with weapons in which they were more skilled. Though convinced of public sympathy, he offered no popular challenge to the senatorial power of his opponents, confining himself to formal political methods. With little talent for such, he was at the mercy of the anti-Scipionic camp. It was Cato's hour. The military command of Lucius was terminated, the treaty with Antiochus severely modified. The so-called trials of the Scipios followed.

In 187, Lucius was charged with failing to account for 500 talents received from the Syrian monarch. Publius may have been accused afterwards, but evidence of the prosecutions is uncertain. If Publius Scipio was not condemned, he was sufficiently disillusioned to leave Rome for Liternum, where he died within a few months. An 'ungrateful Rome' should not have his bones, he growled.

Scipio's death coincided with Cato's term of greatest power. That year he exercised the censorship, ruthlessly revising the lists of knights and senators. All those he judged unworthy by his moral standards, or lacking in proper means, were expelled in an abrasive purge. At the end of his censorship, Cato was fifty. It was to be his last public office, but by no means the end of his influence. For another thirty years and more he would regale the senate with predictable fervour, the arch-opponent of new ideas and old sins.

Meanwhile, a subtler force was working in Africa. It has been shown that the treaty of 201 had given Masinissa of Numidia a claim to such territories of Carthage as had belonged to his ancestors. Within the spirit of the settlement, this may have seemed reasonable, but the clause left room for exploitation. Masinissa set out to make the most of it.

Realistically, the king took account of Roman attitudes. Gratitude between allies had its limits, and Masinissa was far too astute to abuse his luck. Timed at prudent intervals, usually when Rome was elsewhere preoccupied, the Numidian's claims harmonized by remarkable coincidence with ostentatious dem-

onstrations of his support for the Roman cause, or with hints
of unseemly Carthaginian recovery.

Scipio had fixed the Carthaginian frontier after Zama at the
historically familiar Phoenician trench, a line cutting the
modern territory of Tunisia diagonally from Thabraca
(Tabarka) on the northwest coast, to Sfax in the southeast.
Masinissa's first advances, near the profitable Emporia region
on the gulf of Gabes, were outside the new boundary but on
lands the city had long held.

Though Carthage referred the issue of Numidian encroachment to Rome, and a commission was sent to investigate, no
further action was taken by the northern power. A decade
later, Masinissa took armed possession of land in the Bagradas
valley, nearer the African city. Again, appeal to Rome produced no decision. The Numidians stayed put.

In 174, behind a screen of accusations against Carthage, including her alleged implication in a war-plot with Macedon,
Masinissa made another grab. Soon, Carthage could protest
the loss of seventy towns and outposts to her neighbour. Faced
with an urgent appeal for their return, along with lands
usurped earlier, Rome referred the complaint to Masinissa,
demanding explanation.

But a new Romano-Macedonian war was looming, and
Numidia's prompt contribution to the Romans of troops and
provisions blurred the outcome. When Carthage scotched
Masinissa's slanders by offering Rome ships for her campaign,
the king found another charge. The city, he exclaimed, was
contravening peace terms by embarking on naval construction.

The utter defeat of Macedon in 168 left no illusions to those
who had continued to doubt Rome's might. 'For the future,'
wrote the contemporary Polybius, 'nothing remained but to
accept the supremacy of the Romans, and to obey their command.' An overweening sense of mastery, pervading the republic, was reflected in its changing diplomacy. Scipio was
dead. Increasingly, the protective imperialism expressed in his
philosophy gave way to a bullying, ruthless foreign outlook.

Toward Africa, this appeared in a mounting indifference to Carthaginian complaints against Numidia. From 168 to 161, Masinissa concentrated on the gulf of Gabes, annexing the whole of the Emporia to a realm which now ranged from west of Cirta to well into modern Libya. Anger quickened in Carthage. Not only had Rome failed repeatedly to provide redress for injustices, she had actually pronounced on occasions for Numidia.

Carthaginian government was shaken. Seemingly purged of corruption, the aristocratic party which had dominated since Hannibal Barca left had sustained a high order of economic recovery, but backed a forlorn foreign policy. Its view even now was that deference to the Romans would pay off; that Masinissa's ambition was incompatible with the reality of Rome's power, and that eventually the Numidian king would knot his own noose.

Many citizens thought otherwise. A second party favoured *détente* with Masinissa. While no arrangement was likely without concessions to his interest in the city, there were, it was argued, advantages for Carthage in such a course. Masinissa's growing nation, increasingly civilized in outlook, was a potential market of great value for its commercial neighbour. The king's co-operation could hardly prove less dependable than that of Rome.

But the issue was emotional. Obstructing any pro-Numidian policy was the tradition, evolved through centuries, of Carthaginian superiority among the peoples of North Africa. To parley on equal, let alone deferential terms with Masinissa and his 'natives,' was a prospect repugnant to most Carthaginians. Indeed, deference to any power, Rome included, was profoundly at variance with the psyche of a city steeped in independence.

Here lay the basic appeal of a third group, the 'democratic' party of Roman designation, though essentially nationalist. Its leaders, men of rank who based their platform on mass support, spoke alike against the encroachments of Masinissa and the travesty of Roman mediation. Disposed toward self-defence rather than dependance, their advocacy gained adherents with every futile appeal to Rome.

From about 160, Carthaginian government, under popular pressure, adopted a more militant approach to Numidia. The dangers of resisting her intrusions were evident, but the provocation had ceased to be endurable. Among a series of border skirmishes, a raid into usurped territory won acclaim in Carthage for its leader, one Carthalo of the democratic faction. Shortly afterwards, his party formed the government.

Still, the formalities of appeal to Rome were not abandoned. Around 155, Masinissa demonstrated unprecedented audacity, occupying the plains of Souk el Kremis immediately inland of Carthage, well inside the frontier of Scipio. When the outraged Carthaginians informed the Roman senate, yet another commission of inquiry sailed for Africa. It was to prove of grim significance. At its head, eighty-one years of age, travelled Marcus Porcius Cato.

5: 'Delenda est Carthago'

PROBABLY in the summer of 153, the senatorial commission's galley and escort ships stood south for Africa, a voyage into memory for the indomitable old man of Roman politics. Half a century had passed since Cato fought at Zama. A generation had reached middle-age knowing nothing at first hand of the Hannibalic war and its horrors.

Italian trade with Carthage was once more considerable. Pliny described the founders of the city, the Phoenicians, as the inventors of commerce, and it was as a dealer, to be knocked down in the market rather than on the battlefield, that the world of the 2nd century B.C. saw the average Carthaginian. His commercial acumen, execrated by some, was widely envied.

As an alien entrepreneur in the ports of many countries, the Carthaginian was a tempting butt for national humour. Menander, Alexis and Plautus depicted him in plays as a comic turn. In the comedy *Poenulus*, Plautus, who died eighteen years after Zama, portrayed a Carthaginian merchant named Hanno as a self-confessed 'arch-rogue,' ready to turn anything to quick profit: a *gugga*, a shady character living on his quick wits.

Nevertheless, the fictional Hanno had good qualities. Plautus made him a fond father, a kindly relative, a loyal friend. As a pious man, he thanked the gods for his good fortune. So far as he reflected a Roman image of his race, it was, if less than flattering, hardly fraught with animosity.

There were Romans, of course, who took a harsher view. Many old enough to recall the terror and turmoil of Hannibal's invasion retained a bitterness modified but not dispelled by time. Cato had a particularly unforgiving nature. The situation he discovered on returning to Africa stirred a deep resentment in him, a hatred born of the campaigns of his young manhood.

The extent of Carthage's recovery from defeat and the im-
positions of 201 was something of an economic miracle. Within
ten years, the city had felt able to pay off the war indemnity
in full, though an offer to do so had been refused by the
Romans, who preferred to prolong her obligation by the instalments already planned. In part, the revival was made possible by Hannibal's reforms, especially the steps against
corruption.

There had also been an important effort to offset the loss of
Carthaginian colonies in Spain by intensifying the productivity
of the city's fertile, but hitherto underdeveloped, agricultural
lands in Africa. At sea, a vigorous merchant service plied east
to Syrian, Egyptian and Hellenic markets; west to Morocco,
and to Gades (Cadiz) on the Atlantic coast of Spain. Trade
with Italy was brisk. Other factors had played a part in the
revival of prosperity.

Little of the Second Punic War had been fought in Africa.
As Cato might well reflect, it was the Italian lands of the victor
which had endured the greatest depredations. Anomalously,
the lands of the vanquished state had suffered relatively slight
damage. Nor had the manpower losses of Carthage in the
war equalled those of Rome.

Carthaginian armies were largely mercenary, recruited ex-
ternally by officials who travelled widely, often to remote
parts, to contract with local leaders for their warriors. Carthage herself maintained a legion of young men of high birth
to provide an officer reserve. Apart from members of this
group, the casualties of her wars were mainly foreigners.

By contrast, the Roman army still depended on the old
citizen levy, property-holders liable for service of up to six
years at a stretch during sixteen years of manhood. Mobilization not only jeopardized businesses and livelihoods, but also
robbed the state of its most adventurous and patriotic citizens.
Prosperity diminished. As the 2nd century progressed, this
system had come under mounting stress.

When Cato led his commission to Africa, Roman supremacy
of the ancient world, a situation arising more from adept hand-

B*

ling of a series of crises than by deliberate projection, was a
new phenomenon with many probationary problems. It should
not be imagined in terms of the established Roman empire of
the later republic, let alone of the principate. Roman sway in
the autumnal years of Cato was uneven, extemporary, sometimes savagely contested.

In the East, Rome had driven Antiochus from Asia Minor
and abolished the monarchy of Macedon. She had 'liberated'
the Greek states. A rich but weak Egypt looked for her protection. While none doubted that the Romans could deploy
their armies anywhere, the imperial administration of eastern
territories had yet to come. Meanwhile, an exacting patronage
brought protests. Within a few years, the Macedonians and
the Achaean League of Greece would be up in arms.

In the West, Rome's provinces in Corsica, Sicily, Sardinia
and Spain, all captured from Carthage, were sketchily supervised. Of many rebellions and incomplete conquests, the wars
in Spain most severely taxed the Roman government. Their
bearing on its increasing irascibility as the century advanced
is significant.

At first impression, the lands wrested from Carthage in the
Spanish peninsula had looked favourable. Passing down the
eastern coast region, then through the flourishing south toward
Gades, the new masters had found mineral and agricultural
prosperity. Here, where Carthaginian influence was most
marked, the inhabitants had acquired some sophistication.

But when it came to the rest, the outlook was bleak.
Mountains, forests and arid plains, combining with the fierce
reputation of tribes which the Carthaginians had not disturbed,
contributed to a general picture of inhospitability. Roman
geographers described the typical Iberians, as they knew the
peninsula people, as swarthy and tousle-haired, slight, wiry
and pugnacious, practised horsemen and bold, fanatical
fighters.

Some lived in walled towns, others in more primitive
mountain and forest communities. Local pride and independence of spirit were placed by many before their own lives

and the lives of their families. 'Their bodies inured to absti-
nence and toil, their minds composed against death . . . they
prefer war to ease and, should they lack foes without, seek
them within. Rather than betray a secret they will often die
under torment,' declared a Roman commentator.

Stories were told of mothers who murdered their children
to prevent their falling into enemy hands; of prisoners who
killed themselves rather than endure slavedom; of patriots
who chanted songs of victory while being crucified by the
Romans.

Few needed any introduction to violence. For many, including the Celtiberian tribes of the interior and the so-called
Lusitanians of what is now central Portugal, the normal way of
life was warlike and predatory. Sturdily-mounted, trained from
childhood to find their mark with javelin and sling, the Iberians
posed an awesome problem for the Romans. In the areas of
Carthaginian penetration, the tribes had learned military
lessons from their former enemies, including the advantages
of solidarity against a common foe.

Rome's response to this awkward, if temporary, obstacle to
expansion was in keeping with the change in her foreign outlook. Initially, the Roman authorities in Spain, represented
by Sempronius Gracchus, son-in-law of Scipio, had employed
constructive diplomacy with fair success. Later officials
brought a new mood of self-importance and arrogance. Bluster-
ing in their demands, peremptory in use of force, they quickly
provoked hot resistance.

Wild terrain and the unnerving guerilla tactics of the natives
upset the Romans. Normal campaigns devolving on the siege
of a rich city, or the decisive set-piece battle, were their forte;
protracted colonial warfare was another thing. It required regular troops, experienced men led by good generals. It got
neither. Inflated Roman commanders, fearful for their reputa-
tions, resorted to cruelty and treachery to gain their ends.
They only inflamed the opposition.

Within thirty years of the defeat of Carthage, Rome had
drafted 150,000 recruits to Spain, and the worst was still

ahead. In 154, the year before Cato sailed to Africa, the most accomplished and impassioned of Iberian warriors, the Lusitanians, revolted under a dedicated leader named Viriatus. From his mountain hideouts, Viriatus waged remorseless war against the legions, outwitting the best of their captains.

One Roman governor, Galba, was reduced to the particularly contemptible ruse of pretending to grant a truce in order to lure the Lusitanians from the hills to their grazing lands, where he conducted a pitiless massacre. Another general, Caepio, unable to beat Viriatus in battle, plotted his murder by bribery. Joined by the Celtiberians, the Lusitanians fought on.

In Italy, protests against conscription for Spain reached unprecedented proportions, while the plight of sick, often impoverished war veterans contributed to a picture of economic recession. It was against this background of frustration and disgruntlement that Cato's commission exchanged the squalls of Rome for its spell in the sun of the sub-continent. What it found in the lands beyond the blue gulf roused strong emotions in the old chauvinist. Investigation of the African dispute meant travelling through fruitful Carthaginian territories which had never been richer in their produce.

Cato's national pride was affronted by the abundance he saw there, more so by Carthage itself, a city whose manifest prosperity and buoyancy was unclouded by the overseas worries incurred by Rome. Recalling fallen comrades at Zama, and the bloody battles preceding it, it must have seemed to him that Rome had won the war, had gone on to master the Mediterranean, only that Carthage should cream off the benefits.

Embittered by past events, his reflections were exacerbated by the city's approach to arbitration. When the commission insisted that both sides bind themselves in advance to its decision, Masinissa agreed but Carthage dissented. Her experience of Roman mediation scarcely made for confidence. As a token of belated independence, the argument was trivial, yet for Cato it portended danger of the gravest kind.

From the moment the commission returned to Rome, the dispute unsettled, its leader was obsessed with the threat, as he saw it, of a revived Carthage. He is said to have shown the members of the senate a ripe fig, picked in Africa three days earlier, to emphasize the proximity of the old enemy – a continuing enemy, he averred. Thereafter, unable to let it rest, Cato reportedly concluded every speech he made, whatever its subject, with the slogan *'Delenda est Carthago'*–'Carthage must be destroyed.'

6: *Flashpoint*

UNSURPRISINGLY, considering its enormity, Cato's message was not greeted with rapturous applause in Rome. Even today, when weapon capabilities have made mass destruction commonplace, the idea of blotting out a great city – not in war or under dire provocation, but as an act of cold-blooded political expediency – accords more with fantasy than reality.

Applied to ancient Carthage, with her uniquely formidable ramparts, it verged on the preposterous.

All the same, the proposal found a following. That it was not dismissed out of hand says much for Cato's personal standing, and perhaps more about the diminishing equability of Roman response to foreign problems. Little is known of complexions in the senate at this period, but the repetitious obstinacy of the old man's propaganda suggests both grim hope on his part and lack of popularity.

The following year, 152, Cato was snubbed by the dispatch of a further commission to Africa, this time headed by a prominent opponent of his views, Publius Scipio Nasica ('Scipio of the Pointed Nose'). A close kinsman of 'Africanus,' Scipio Nasica had no cause to love the Cato faction. According to one source, he parodied the notorious 'Carthage must be destroyed' exhortation by concluding his own addresses to the senate with the words, 'And *I* think that Carthage should be left alone.'

At all events, he returned to Italy with inflammatory news for the Catoists, having persuaded Masinissa to yield some disputed ground to Carthage. Scipio Nasica did not deny the renewed vigour of the African city, but took the view, not original, that a buoyant rival was essential to Rome's inner strength, to her traditional virility which, he claimed, would degenerate – indeed, was so doing – without competition.

Another strategic possibility, seen by some as a stronger

incentive to pre-emptive action than Cato's fears, cast Masinissa as the main threat, Carthage being the economic key the king needed to possess an African nation of world account. By this reckoning, the pro-Numidian party in Carthage, not her popular movement, was the real barometer of trouble ahead for Rome.

The support for these arguments in 152 is conjectural. Nothing known suggests that Cato's campaign made much ground in its first year. Certainly, it did not discourage Carthage, at last a modest beneficiary of Roman mediation, from further appeals to Rome for help against Numidia. Then, in 151, a number of diverse events combined with dramatic force.

For twelve hectic months the Roman legions in Spain had been in almost ceaseless combat. Reports told of countless deaths; of the impossibility of defeating the Celtiberians. Disillusion was widespread. Officers refused to volunteer for the peninsula; veteran soldiers declined to march with their leaders. To the consternation of a society which regarded army service as a cause for pride, the number of youths evading enlistment was so great that punishment became impossible.

For the first time in a century, the senate had lost its grip on men and methods.

At the same time, Rome complained that Carthage was rebuilding an army and naval force. The African city's dispute with Numidia had reached flashpoint, embassies and counter-embassies scuttling to Italy for crisis talks. Probably, a Carthaginian army of some size had evolved from the territorial skirmishes coinciding with the resurgence of the popular party. Half a century of Numidian encroachment underlined the need for it. Fighting ships were less important. Masinissa's was not a seafaring nation, and it is doubtful if Carthage projected a large fleet.

In a calmer moment, the formal protest Rome presented at these breaches of a somewhat dated treaty might have led to satisfaction. But the hour was fraught for both sides. That year, Carthage was due to pay the final instalment of the war indemnity. The knowledge that she would then have a substantial surplus revenue to devote to other things, possibly armaments, did nothing to relieve the trauma occasioned in Rome by bitter Spanish setbacks. Suddenly, the Roman climate, xenophobic, vindictive, favoured Cato's call for violent action.

In Carthage, an atmosphere of mounting crisis overrode Roman strictures as public indignation centred on the opprobrious Numidians. Late in 151, the government, losing patience, expelled the leading members of the pro-Masinissa faction in the city and, prompted by Carthalo and other fervent nationalists, insultingly rejected the king's protests. The popular party denied his envoys entry to Carthage and even attacked them on their way home.

Having threatened for decades, the conflict exploded.

Masinissa promptly attacked a town of Carthaginian connection named Oroscopa, while forces under Carthalo and another captain, Hasdrubal, marched against the king. Masinissa was now almost ninety. Anticipating his death, the princes he had ruled with patriarchal rigidity jockeyed for the dynastic struggle they saw ahead. Two of his sons joined Hasdrubal, doubtless hopeful of repayment in kind later.

Weakened by the desertions, Masinissa withdrew to a region remote from Carthaginian supply routes. Confidently, Hasdrubal followed. A number of preliminary engagements had gone his way and he sought the major battle. It remains, in its obscurity, one of the phantom epics of Africa, remarked chiefly for the presence of a notable spectator : a young Roman officer seeking elephants for the Spanish war.

The son of a distinguished soldier (Aemilius Paullus, conqueror of Macedon) and adopted member of the Scipionic family, the talented Scipio Aemilianus had already won a name for intrepidity in Spain when he found himself perched on a hillside in North Africa watching a sprawling battle on the plain below. He relished the experience. 'It was a privilege,' he declared later, 'such as only two had enjoyed before me, Zeus from the top of Mount Ida and Poseidon from Samothrace, in the Trojan War.'

Masinissa, grey from more years even than Cato, commanded

the Numidians in person, riding without saddle or stirrups in the native style. But the day proved indecisive, and the Roman witness was at length asked to mediate. Negotiations faltered over the deserters, Masinissa demanding the surrender of his sons, the Carthaginians refusing to co-operate. Imprudently, since the terrain itself was hostile, Hasdrubal postponed breaking camp in expectation of further talks.

They failed to materialize. Instead, the Carthaginians discovered that the artful Numidian had exploited the delay to blockade their return routes. Trapped in barren country, Hasdrubal's troops were first weakened by famine then swept by epidemic. In the end, they agreed to purchase a passage by surrendering their arms and the deserters, and promising an indemnity.

Even so, disaster awaited the survivors. As they trudged defencelessly from camp, Masinissa's horsemen harried them savagely, leaving few to reach safety. The affair might have been planned to suit Cato. By embarking on war against Numidia in contravention of the treaty of 201, Carthage had absolved Rome of her legal obligation as co-signatory. By losing that war, and her army to boot, Carthage had left herself naked. Walls she possessed, but no battalions to man them.

Also, she had reinforced the old bogey of Carthaginian perfidy. Romans on the whole might not share Cato's hatred of Carthage, but they did regard her people with mistrust. Like Plautus's Hanno, they were thought to be tricky rogues. Trickery could be amusing in a pedlar, but when it came to breaking treaties the legalistic Roman had a meagre sense of humour. The public, as one Roman avouched, was not discriminatory in what it believed about the Punic race.

By 150, 'Destroy Carthage!' had ceased to seem an outrageous slogan. Against the drift of sentiment, Scipio Nasica warned of the need to have regard for world opinion. But to many minds the destruction of an untrustworthy city would be a salutary message to the world, succinct in any tongue: a timely counter to wrong ideas which might be drawn from the intransigence of Spanish savages.

Contrary to recruiting problems apropos of Spain, raising an army for the seemingly profitable picnic of demolishing a rich and cultivated state was all too easy. 80,000 Italians, undeceived by official secrecy about their destination, quickly volunteered for the campaign. It could hardly have come at a more opportune moment. Masinissa, having smashed the Carthaginian army, was fast approaching the end of his own life.

In the struggle for succession which must follow, Numidia would be ill-placed either to exploit the demise of her rival or to contest a Roman stake in Africa.

How far the ruthlessness of Roman intentions toward Carthage was part of a wider strategy of supremacy, or in fact a crude reaction in the absence of any real policy, is questionable. The ancient world was divided in opinion. According to Polybius, one school of thought held the assault on Carthage an astute and far-sighted action on Rome's part, while others saw it as the brutal aberration of a normally civilized nation, a treacherous and profane act.

Its immensity was not doubted. The sands of Punic history were running out.

7: *Dido and the Voyagers*

LEGEND has it that Carthage was founded in the 9th century B.C. by a princess of Tyre named Elissa, or Dido. When Dido's brother, Pygmalion, became king, the princess married her uncle, Acherbas, the wealthiest member of the royal house. Coveting his fortune, Pygmalion had Acherbas murdered, but Dido escaped to sea with the riches and her followers.

According to the story, told with several variations, Dido sailed to Cyprus where the high priest of the Semitic goddess Astarte agreed to join her on condition that his family should be granted the priesthood in perpetuity of any colony founded. A number of sacred prostitutes embarked with him, to provide women for the men and, in time, regenerate the company.

In Justin's version of the legend, Dido went to Africa where

finding that the people of those parts were well disposed to strangers, and liked buying and selling, she agreed to buy a piece of land, so much as could be encompassed by the hide of an ox, on which to rest her weary companions. This hide she cut into narrow strips that they might encircle a large plot, which was called Byrsa, that is the Hide.

Like Utica, a colony already thriving on the coast to the west, Dido's foundation prospered. But so great was the reputation of the princess's beauty (runs the fable) that one native chieftain insisted on marrying her, failing which he promised to make war on the settlement. At this, Dido had a huge pyre built on the outskirts of the colony, climbed on to it sword-in-hand, and, swearing faithfulness to her dead husband, took her own life.

Thus Dido burned. The story, owing much to Greek elaboration, need not be taken literally. Dido, or Elissa, are not historically authenticated persons, deriving respectively from Semitic words meaning 'beloved' and 'goddess.'

The ox hide anecdote appears repeatedly in founding legends, being told of Assassin settlement in Persia, Saxon settlement in England, and even of English settlement in America. Again, *byrsa* meant an ox hide to the Greeks, but the Phoenician colonists, presumably christening the camp site in their own tongue, more likely used the word *bozra*, a stronghold – this corrupted in time by Greek usage.

Yet there are points of factual interest in the legend. Though traditional dates for Phoenician settlement are suspect, archaeological evidence suggests that Utica was indeed older than Carthage; nor is there reason to doubt that the settlers were Tyrians. Indubitably, they hailed from that land of which Tyre was a leading community, Phoenicia, or Canaan as its own people knew it.

The Phoenicians, a Semitic people closely related to the Hebrews, had turned to seafaring early in their history, when they migrated from the Negeb to a narrow strip of coast in the region of modern Lebanon and Palestine. Afflicted by powerful land enemies, the Phoenicians depended heavily on maritime skills for survival and prosperity. Tyre, a rocky island a few hundred yards off-shore, was able to survive long sieges thanks to her many ships.

When the fall of Cnossos in the 14th century ended the long-standing danger posed by Cretan fleets to traffic in the sea lanes south of Greece, Tyrian captains ventured further and further west. The merchandise they brought back increased the city's wealth and influence. Ezekiel described Tyre as 'the renowned city which wast strong in the sea,' a brilliant market for commodities from all parts of the known world.

Isaiah called her 'the crowning city, whose merchants are princes, whose traffickers are the honourable of the earth.'

To Tyre came spices from Arabia, amber from the Baltic, foodstuffs from Judaea, linen from Egypt, copper from Cyprus and, increasingly as her ships reached the limits of the western sea, precious metals from Tarshish, or Tartessus, in the south of Spain. Here, on the very brink of the unknown, the ocean without end, were the fabulous mines, rich in gold, silver, tin and other minerals, familiar to Solomon and his neighbours.

Here berthed the biblical 'ships of Tarshish,' the long-distance freighters which plied a 4,000-mile return journey from the Levant. At Phoenician Gadir (from which stemmed the Roman *Gades*, hence Cadiz), the easterners established a colony handy for the silver mines of the Sierra Morena, and other works. Acquired cheaply from the natives, sold expensively in the east, the metals not only brought wealth to Phoenicia's home cities but helped finance settlements in Africa, Cyprus, Sicily, and elsewhere.

Intermediate stations between Phoenicia and Spain were imperative. Ancient seafarers of the Mediterranean, vulnerable to rough weather in their narrow oarships, primitive in navigation and reluctant to sail at night, seldom ventured far from land. Their method of traversing seas was either to follow the most suitable coast, or to hop from island to island. Normally, they anchored during the late part of the day, often looking to the shore for rest and refreshment.

In the circumstances, the obvious course to Tarshish from the Levant was along the relatively direct coastline of North Africa rather than by the devious boundary of Europe. Island-hopping was only practicable in the eastern part of the Mediterranean. It was also true that the pirate swarms of competing maritime states, especially those of Greece, were less prolific in the south than in the Ionian, Aegean and Cretan seas.

Feeling their way along the northern rim of the sub-continent, the Phoenicians discovered immense stretches of shore untouched by eastern progress, or by the tides of human migration disrupting much of Europe. Time had stood still in North Africa, a world isolated by formidable deserts to landward, to seaward by a face of inhospitable cliffs and dunes with few natural harbours.

It was a wild, awesome realm abounding in great animals: elephants, lions, bears, panthers (now extinct in the north, but prolific on the coastlands in antiquity). The people of the region, living in small tribes, largely nomadic, remained in the stone age of material development. At first, disunified and amenable to enticement with cheap commercial products, they were less an obstacle to settlement on the whole than the land itself.

Vast tracts of barren and parched coast encouraged no more than the establishment of small communications posts. These were frequent. The Phoenicians organized anchorages at regular intervals, possibly every thirty miles or so. But few became places of any real permanency. Only in limited areas, where scope for cultivation coincided with harbourage, would settlement prosper. Outstanding among these was northern Tunisia.

In this region, reaching fondly toward the toe of Italy, fertile lands and an equable climate soon attracted the attention of the voyagers. Coastal conditions were suitable to the growth of a variety of fruit trees; corn, though susceptible to inter-mittent droughts, grew well on the inland vales. Halfway be-tween Tarshish and the Levant, the gulf of Tunis plainly beckoned the early Phoenicians.

Strategically, its proximity to the Sicilian narrows, dominat-ing the passage between eastern and western spheres, was portentous.

Of the Phoenician settlements which attained any size in North Africa, most were in this area. The site of Carthage, the 'ship at anchor,' was typically Phoenician in its choice; indeed, remarkably similar to that of Tyre. Its most sheltered beach, on the bay of Kram, probably served as the earliest anchorage. Nearby, the settlers placed their sacred enclosure, the sanctu-ary of Tanit; built their first defences on the plateau of the Byrsa; planned their man-made harbours.

The name Carthage (Greek *Karchēdon*) derives from the Semitic *Kirjath-Hadeschath*, or 'New Town' – new in relation either to the motherland of the migrants, or the neighbouring and older settlement of Utica. The time generally accepted by the ancients for the birth of the city was thirty-eight years

before the first Olympiad, that is 814, though the earliest remains found on the site post-date this by a century.

It is yet another hundred years before Carthage begins to
appear in written history. By then, the colony was already
prosperous. Herodotus, harking back to 650, offered the tradition of a then mature Carthage, rich and envied. Before the
close of the 6th century, her fame was such that the Persian
emperor Cambyses, having conquered Egypt, dispatched an
army from that country to seize the jewel of the coast for his
diadem. Heading optimistically west, the Persian troops
marched into the Libyan desert and vanished – as the early
years of Carthage were to vanish from record – without trace.

While the 'New Town' grew, the old Phoenicia declined.
Tyre, repeatedly menaced by the warlords of Assyria and
Babylon, had weakened long before Carthage was strong
enough to bring relief. Instead, she succoured refugees from
the motherland and prepared to defend *herself*, not from the
distant land-powers of Asia, or even primarily from local
tribes, but from an insidious seaborne peril which, from about
750, threatened to overwhelm Semitic settlement in the west.

Benefiting from the misfortunes of metropolitan Phoenicia,
Greece had edged steadily to the fore in westering colonization.
Generation by generation, fleets of hardy, resourceful Greek
migrants, impelled by overcrowding in mainland Hellas, by
Persian encroachment on Ionia, by their own questing spirits,
descended on the shores of Italy, Sicily, Provence. Some even
settled in Spain and Cyrenaica.

Everywhere, Phoenician colonization was endangered. The
Greeks were as adroit at sea as the Semites, readier to turn to
piracy and war where commercial competition failed. One by
one, the Phoenician settlements gave way until Tunisia, encircled, at last produced a challenger. Alone against the ubiquitous enemy, Carthage was to come of age violently.

8: *The Siceliots*

OF the incentives urging Carthage to militant leadership of the western Phoenicians, the most immediate was Greek encroachment in Sicily. Phoenician control of the Sicilian ports, hence guardianship of the narrows between the island and Carthage, had long held the eastern approach to a select, if somewhat unscrupulous, sailing club.

Greek geographers looked back on the western Mediterranean as a Phoenician lake, a vast preserve on which foreigners trespassed at their peril. To be caught there, declared Strabo, recalling Eratosthenes, was to suffer instant death by drowning. The *Odyssey* gave the early Phoenicians a bad name. They were, in the eyes of the western Greeks, 'famous for their ships,' but 'greedy men,' robbing stealthily, ingloriously.

To the admirers of Heroic Greece, piracy and plunder in themselves assigned no stigma. Hellas was born a sea-brigand. What aroused the 'anti-semitic' indignation of many Greeks, especially the nobility, was the despised commercial instinct of the Phoenicians and their profitable operations west of Greece – a march stolen on a race with a geographic head-start.

Eastern Sicily, fertile and close to Greece, was a natural bridgehead in the westering movement from Hellas. Among the first Greek settlements there were Naxos (734), at the foot of Mount Etna, and Syracuse (733), further south.

At about the same time, Messana and Rhegium were founded either side of the straits of Messina, giving access by sea to western Italy. The Phocaeans of Ionia, reputedly the best long-distance sailors among the Greeks, pushed on to found Massilia (Marseilles) and several posts on the Spanish coast. Of these, the most southerly competed at Tarshish.

In Sicily, new Greek colonies followed, in the north at Himera, in the south at Selinus. The latter, less than a hundred miles from Carthaginian Africa, raised a serious possibility that the Phoenicians could lose their western hold on the island. In such a situation, the Carthaginians were convinced, the Greeks would dominate the western sea, cut the lanes to Sardinia and menace Carthage herself.

A concerted attempt to drive the Phoenicians from Sicily was soon to come. The third decade of the 6th century saw the Siceliots, as the Sicilian Greeks were known, reinforced by bands of new Greek settlers from Rhodes and the Dorian port of Cnidos, in Asia Minor. Under a leader named Pentathlos, the Rhodians and Cnidians established themselves at Lilybaeum, in the extreme west of the island, contiguous to the ultimate Phoenician stronghold of Motya.

At last, having submitted tamely to repeated intrusions, the Phoenicians resisted. In conjunction with a native tribe of Sicily, the Elymians, they defied Pentathlos and destroyed Lilybaeum.

Carthage now adopted a policy of intervention to the north. Historical sources are still scant, but it seems that some time following the repulse of Pentathlos a Carthaginian chief called Malchus (the Greeks may have mistaken the Semitic word *melek*, or king, for a proper name) led a force to Sicily to strengthen Phoenician positions there. Motya, the seagirt fortress of the west, was reinforced.

Malchus sailed on to Sardinia. There, Carthage helped to sustain the Phoenician settlements through a stormy period. The natives were hostile and Greek pirates prowled the coast. In 560, the Phocaean Greeks established a strong colony in Corsica, their fifty-oared warships plundering adjacent Sardinia and her sea trade.

To beat the pirates, Carthage joined forces with Etruria, the Italian land facing Corsica, whose ships had also been set upon. The Etruscans, an assertive, advanced people, were redoubtable warriors but lacked a large fleet. As a check to Greek expansion, the alliance with maritime Carthage was potent.

Sweeping the northern islands, a combined Carthaginian-Etruscan armada engaged the pirate navy. The Phocaeans, outnumbered, put up a savage fight, their big warships driving the allies before them. But their losses were crucial. Reduced to 20 vessels, a third of their original number, the Greeks abandoned Corsica to the Etruscans and soon withdrew from southern Spain.

Carthage was well served. Direct threat to Sardinia was averted; Carthaginian monopoly of Tarshish restored. The wealth from the region was vital to her new role. Leadership of the western Phoenicians had brought not only economic and political dominance but a military burden disproportionate to her population.

Malchus had led a citizen levy, the characteristic army of ancient states. For defensive purposes, and short campaigns, the system was adequate, but the demands of overseas commitments put it under heavy strain. Economically, it made better sense to devote revenue in part to hiring troops beyond the city rather than waste the lives and energies of a specialized community whose talents were better used creating wealth.

Military reform is traditionally ascribed to a luminary named Mago, whose reign or magistracy (it is uncertain when the early kings of Carthage were replaced by suffetes, or magistrates) embraced the enlistment of forces from dependent states and the use of foreign mercenaries.

Carthaginians still held command, while an élite corps of citizens – known by the Greeks as the Sacred Band – was retained to stiffen and inspire the new armies. Equipped and trained as heavy infantry, in the manner of Greek hoplites, the Sacred Band complemented the early hired troops, Libyans and Spaniards, who fought lightly-armed, sometimes as cavalry.

The system was effective. By Mago's death, Sardinia had been thoroughly consolidated while the Siceliots accepted Carthaginian interest in western Sicily. Many Greeks, misrepresented by a bellicose minority, were content to trade with the Phoenicians, some even to conduct their businesses in Phoenician colonies. The obverse was also true.

Indeed, when a Spartan prince named Dorieus threatened to upset the status quo by settling in the far west of Sicily at the end of the 6th century, he received no encouragement from the Greek colonies. Shunned by the Siceliots, his followers were overwhelmed by the Phoenicians, Dorieus killed.

In these circumstances it was not impossible that the western Mediterranean could have witnessed a gradual merger of cultures, encouraged by commerce, in which Carthage (increasingly exposed to Greek manners, drawn north by the Etruscan pact) might in time have shed her eastern heritage. That she became, as it happened, isolationist, a uniquely individual force, owed much to two early developments. Each was rooted in the fortunes of eastern Greece.

Here, on the shores of the Aegean, radical changes had come about in politics. With increasing commercial prosperity, the old Greek states had acquired a strong middle or trading class which, independent of the soil, was also independent of aristocratic landlords. Enviously, the poorer classes had stirred themselves to question the yoke of the nobility. Finally, popular movements had tumbled aristocracies and kingdoms.

In ultimate form, such movements had already produced the democracies of Athens and some other states. Elsewhere, revolution had resulted in a form of government where more or less popular leaders held power as new autocrats. Terminologically distinguished from the old kings as tyrants – the new form of rule being a *turannos*, or tyranny – many of these rulers were enlightened men. Others, prevailing at length, brought tyranny to disrepute.

Meanwhile, the Siceliots, clinging to customs brought with them from former times, lagged in development. Until the beginning of the 5th century, most Siceliot states were controlled by the nobility. Then, as a fresh wave of Asiatic Greeks fled west from the Persians, the situation abruptly changed.

New ideas, introduced by the migrants, who included passionate revolutionaries, threw the Greek cities of Sicily into a turmoil of instability and violence. From the ferment emerged a breed of tyrants of the worst kind: egotistic, ruthless, destructive in their conquests. Among the first, both controlling cities on the south coast, were Gelon of Gela and Theron of Acragas.

Gelon, to dominate this baneful partnership, had served his apprenticeship as lieutenant to another tyrant, Hippocrates. The training was a thorough one. In alliance with Theron, he first seized Syracuse, the finest port in eastern Sicily and the key to communications with the east. Making this his new capital, and the base for a growing fleet, he then turned his gaze west.

His ambition frightened not only the Sicilian Phoenicians but a good many Siceliots. Among the latter was the ruler of northern Himera, Terillos, a friend of the Carthaginian family of Mago, the influential Magonids. When Terillos, driven from his city by Gelon's ally Theron, appealed to Carthage, a major confrontation seemed probable.

A second eastern development heightened the crisis. The new century had opened with a situation of cold war between Athens, a supporter of the Ionian rebels, and Persia's western bureau at Sardis. In the summer of 490, a year after Gelon came to power in Sicily, the Persian emperor Darius assembled one of the largest armadas then seen to impress his might on Athens and eastern Greece.

Marathon, an Athenian victory against the odds, won time for Hellas but made a greater invasion inevitable. Xerxes, son of Darius, prepared to conquer Greece. In 481, enslavement to Persia seeming imminent, the threatened Greek states asked Gelon to rally to the motherland. He did not respond. Terillos had barely been exiled from Himera. Gelon expected trouble of his own, from Carthage.

But if the tyrant was ill-placed to reinforce mainland Greece, more significant was the knowledge that Greece could not assist Gelon. How far Carthage was swayed by this is debateable. The later Greek writer Diodorus Siculus claimed an arrangement between Persia and Carthage to synchronize their attacks. Others disputed it. One thing seems certain: the eastern Phoenicians, who assisted Xerxes's preparations, were unlikely to have kept Carthage in ignorance of his plans. If she meant to tackle Gelon, now was the moment.

The Carthaginian force entrusted with restoring Terillos was the strongest yet fielded by the city, and the first whose composition is detailed. Apart from Libyans and Iberians, it contained Sardinians, Corsicans and 'Helisyki,' the last obscure in origin. A member of the Magonids, Hamilcar, commanded the expedition.

Greek historians, gross in exaggerating the strength of their enemies, numbered his force at 300,000. Divided by ten, a more realistic figure may be obtained. Even then, part of the army, seemingly its cavalry, was lost when a storm struck the transport ships. Rounding the western end of Sicily without interception, the rest of the fleet put in at Panormus (Palermo), roughly equidistant from pro-Carthaginian Selinus, southwest, and hostile Himera, some fifty miles east.

Gelon, warned by Theron of Hamilcar's approach, was ready with his army. The opposing forces marched on Himera from Panormus and Syracuse, encamping beyond the walls, the invasion fleet beached in the vicinity. Marginally outnumbered, the tyrant compensated with a cunning stroke.

Hamilcar called on Selinus to replace the cavalry lost at sea. Learning of this, Gelon dispatched a body of his own horse to keep the rendezvous. Deceiving the guard on the Carthaginian fleet, the Syracusian cavalry gained their camp and burnt the beached ships. It was a demoralizing blow for Hamilcar's mercenaries. They fought stubbornly but never regained the initiative.

The fate of their general is hazy. According to Carthaginian report, recalled by Herodotus, on perceiving the battle lost Hamilcar threw himself into a sacrificial fire lit to appease the Phoenician gods, thus emulating Dido. Alternatively, he was said to have been cut down by the impostors who fired the ships. Few of his men escaped death or capture.

Carthage was stunned by the bad news. Her most ambitious intervention to date in Greek affairs, Himera would have been costly enough as a victory. As a defeat, it was exorbitant. Gelon had now to be bought off with silver. His price was more than fifty tons of it.

To the north, the Etruscans were losing ground to the Italian Greeks. In the east, Salamis had proved a Persian debacle. It was a time for licking burnt fingers. Prudently, the Carthaginians fell back in Sicily on Motye and the far west, leaving the Siceliots to resolve their own arguments. Revenge would come later. At the moment, Africa, for all its wild wastes, seemed the safest place.

9: *The Africa Enterprise*

NAVAL losses inflicted by Gelon; the diminution of northern trade, especially the import of corn and oil; the need to accumulate reserves against the prospect of renewed war – a variety of factors stimulated Carthaginian interest in the hitherto neglected hinterland. Poetically, the change of strategic emphasis was described by one writer (Chrysostom of Antioch) as 'transforming the Carthaginians into Africans.'

Apart from its northern fringe, Africa mystified the ancient world. Egypt had encountered the Nubians of the Upper Nile, fought the Ethiopians – the 'dark-faced people'–, probed the Libyan wilderness. Beyond, in an imagined domain of monsters and sorcerers, the gods held nocturnal revels and the sun retired: so thought Homer.

While the coasts of Andalusia, Italy and the intervening islands presented obvious attractions to Carthaginian travellers, the aspect inland of their adopted shore was forbidding. To the west, the Tellian Atlas formed an almost unbroken barrier between the sea and the interior as far as the straits of Gibraltar. To the east, the coastal plains, themselves less daunting, were bounded by swamps and the wastes of the Hamada. Predatory beasts roamed a jungle of wild olives and mastic trees.

The people encountered in North Africa were known by the Greeks as Libyans, later as Berbers from the Latin *Barbarus*. A group of tribes sharing a basically common tongue, they were scattered widely between Egypt and the Atlantic coast. South of the Atlas, they bordered on black preserves. To the north, through the early history of settlement, they held sway to the outskirts of the coastal towns.

Little is known of the race other than that it was white and nomadic, subsisting by stockbreeding, hunting and exploiting the black tribes. Inured to a harsh existence, its people were fierce and austere, not dissimilar, it seems, to the Tuareg of modern times. Until the epoch of Himera, they had been sufficiently strong in Tunisia to exact ground-rent from Carthage.

Thereafter, the city set about subduing its neighbours with urgency. The chronology of her African expansion is imprecise. Some acquisitions may have occurred in the 6th century; some not until the 4th. Nevertheless, by far the greatest surge of activity attached to that part of the 5th century following Himera.

It was led by the family most anxious to efface the humility, namely the Magonids, in particular by a son of Hamilcar named Hanno. Hanno lost no time. In the space of a few decades, Carthage had dominated the easterly peninsula of Cape Bon, conquered an area of the hinterland (including the Medjerda and Siliana plains) approximating to the most fertile part of modern Tunisia, raised villas and farmsteads in the wilderness.

The annexed regions were of two kinds: those immediate to Carthage, including the isthmus and Cape Bon peninsula, counted as city land; the more distant as subject territories. Their inhabitants seem not to have been enslaved as a general rule. Adopting, at least in part, the culture of their masters, they became, again in Greek parlance, Libyphoenicians.

By the end of the century, visitors would express amazement at the fecundity of a countryside transformed by fruit trees, vines, almond, pomegranate and cereals. Land experts had supervised the reclamation. One of them, an official with the favoured name of Mago, was celebrated for a treatise on agriculture which, translated, became a standard Roman source. 'Above all writers,' declared the agriculturist Columella, 'we honour Mago the Carthaginian, father of husbandry.' Varro cited the work as the highest authority in its field.

Control of the interior reinforced the authority of Carthage in Phoenician coastal settlements. Though numerous, these had not on the whole attained much size. Few could be dignified

Ruins at Tyre.

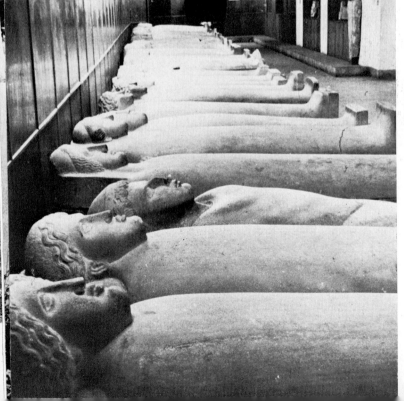

Phoenician sar-
cophagi found
at Sidon.

The fall of Carthage — 19th century artist's impression. Mary Evans Picture Library

(A) Coin attributed to Hamilcar. Late 3rd century BC.
(B) Coin attributed to Hannibal. Late 3rd century BC. Minted in Spain.
(C) Coin of King Masinissa of Numidia 202 — 148 BC.
(D) Silver Denarius of the Roman Republic (c. 105 BC) showing Scipio. British Museum

as cities in any sense. Some had grown into modest townships with markets attracting the surrounding tribes; others remained no more than trading stations, possibly occupied seasonally.

The most easterly of the dependencies was on the gulf of Sidra, or Sirte, where Tripolitania borders Cyrenaica. Here, Phoenician territory abutted Greek settlement. Sallust told how two teams of runners, Carthaginian and Greek, competed to decide the point of the frontier. This, it was agreed, should be fixed where the opposing runners met, each team having started from the last outpost on its own land.

According to the story, the Carthaginian champions, the brothers Philaeni, covered the greater distance, but the Greeks disputed their performance. At this, the two brothers declared themselves ready to be buried alive at the site of their achievement provided it was acknowledged the frontier. The sacrifice was accepted. At all events, a spot known as the altars of the Philaeni marked the limits of Hellenism in Africa until the end of antiquity.

However the name originated, the legend has significance, for fanatical selflessness in public duty – a quality oddly set beside material acquisitiveness – was widely accepted as a trait of Punic character. Closely linked with spiritual beliefs placing mortal life at a discount, it was not irrelevant to pioneering Africa – a continent whose dangers terrified intrepid men.

The chief Carthaginian dependency between the gulf of Sidra and the westerly gulf of Gabes was Leptis, later known as Leptis Major (Leptis Minor was on the east coast of Tunisia). Like other settlements in Tripolitania, Leptis thrived on trade with the interior. Here tribesmen familiar with the desert trails to the Niger brought emeralds, chalcedony, carbuncles and gold dust to exchange for cheap goods from Carthage.

And from here, in all probability, Carthaginian merchant adventurers mounted their first Saharan expeditions.

So attractive were the valuables from Nigeria and Senegal that nothing could dissuade some traders from seeking the distant and myth-shrouded treasure hoards. The road to Eldo-

C

rado confirmed its reputation. Native trails, leading south to the immemorial Saharan junction of Fezzan, continued south-west by Tassili round the Ahaggar, thence by the wastes of the Tanezrouft and Adrar to the Niger, emerging somewhere in the depths of modern Mali.

Though less extensive than today, the desert was treacher-ous. Crossing the Tanezrouft involved travelling four days without water. Camels, little used for transport until Christian times, were unavailable. Instead, the ancients used light chariots drawn by horses with water-skins slung beneath their bellies. The ability to tolerate thirst was imperative. One Carth-aginian explorer, another Mago, was said to have crossed the desert three times without drinking, though which region he crossed is uncertain.

From Fezzan, a bold western traveller might also reach Egypt and the Sudan without touching Greek Cyrenaica, by braving the sand trails of Kufra and Tibesti. Unfortunately, the indi-vidual exploits of these earliest of trans-Saharan adventurers are lost in time. Only an occasional hint in ancient literature remains to convey the danger from desert tribes, the mon-strous apparitions (heat hallucinations?) reputed to exist among the burning dunes, the plight of travellers held prisoner by pigmies of the great swamps, the impact of bush and jungle on explorers two millennia before the age of David Livingstone 'discovered' tropical Africa.

Despite the perils, trade grew with the interior. The im-portance of desert cargoes to Carthage is witnessed by the substantial customs dues her treasury gained from Leptis: the equivalent, at one period, of a ton of silver per month.

Other business flourished on the coast between Sidra and Gabes. Fishing was important, both as a food industry and for the production of a purple dye much demanded by the ancients. Offshore lay the island of Meninx, claimed as the home of the Lotus Eaters of the *Odyssey*. Fertile and temperate, it was highly cultivated.

Beyond the gulf of Gabes, where the coast turned north toward Cape Bon, the eastern seabord came under close supervision from Carthage. Among the places on this coast were Thaenae, Acholla, Thapsus, Leptis Minor and Hadrumetum, the last the largest, possessing a developed harbour complex. Directly accessible by land from the metropolis, this coast attracted Carthaginian residents. Hannibal Barca was among those to own a house at Thapsus.

Some time in the 5th century, a handsome town was built at modern Dar Essafi, near the point of Cape Bon, but the west side of the peninsula, facing Carthage, was barren of settlements. The rest of the African empire lay to the Atlantic side of the capital.

Proceeding from Carthage toward the straits of Gibraltar, the older city of Utica was quickly encountered at the water's edge. Today, the site is inland, attesting the changes in the coast near Cape Farina. Utica's status appears to have varied from senior and privileged dependent to partner of Carthage, though not always a constant one. To her west, a string of anchorages, some established by Carthage, some of earlier origin, served the Andalusian and Moroccan trade.

First of importance was Hippo Acra (Bizerta), whose physiographical appeal to seamen was strong from an early date. From Hippo to the gulf of Bougie, or thereabouts, the Numidians held the interior, their median stronghold at Cirta. On the coast, Carthaginian Iol, near modern Algiers, was of probable importance in the 5th century.

Finally, at the gateway of the ancient sea, Tingi, commemorated in Tangier, looked out on horizons wreathed in speculation – horizons Carthage was determined to investigate.

10: *Into the Ocean*

IF one way of reaching gold was across the Sahara, another was round it : that is, by sea down the Atlantic coast. Logically, the westerly colonization of North Africa prefaced settlement on the Moroccan shores beyond Tangier, a development strongly backed by the expansionist Hanno. It was, like all enterprise in the far west, a subject of restricted information so far as Carthage's competitors were concerned. Greek ignorance of the sphere confirms the level of trade secrecy.

Pindar, writing at the very moment Carthage was investigating the Atlantic shores of Africa and Europe, declared the straits of Gibraltar – the Pillars of Hercules, as the Greeks had it – the limits of the accessible world. Beyond, in Hellenic mythology, lay the Garden of Hesperides where Hercules, winning the golden apples, achieved apotheosis.

By the second half of the 5th century, Herodotus had caught word of the beginnings of Moroccan trade :

> *The Carthaginians speak of a part of Libya (Africa) and its people beyond the straits of Gibraltar. On reaching this land they unload their goods and place them on the beach, then they retire to their ships and make signals. The natives, sighting the smoke, come down to the shore, place a quantity of gold beside the goods, and in turn retire. The Carthaginians come ashore again. If they deem the gold sufficient payment for the goods, they collect it and sail away; if not, they go aboard again and wait until the natives have added more gold. There is no deception. The Carthaginians never touch the gold, nor the natives the goods, until both are satisfied.*

This is the earliest known description of dumb barter, a procedure noted in West Africa during the middle ages, and again as recently as the Victorian era. Essentially a first step in trade relationships, no doubt it had been superseded by closer contacts in Morocco when Herodotus wrote. The immense profitability of the exchange to the Carthaginians was a powerful incentive to secure the sea route by colonization. Accordingly, about the middle of the 5th century, Hanno embarked on a celebrated voyage west.

The expedition, of both settlement and discovery, was remarkable not only for the romance engendered – a mixture of Nuno Tristão and Sinbad the Sailor – but as the origin of the only substantial Carthaginian document to have survived in something like its true form. Hanno had an account of his adventures engraved on a stele in the temple of Baal Hammon at Carthage. Later, probably in the 4th century, a version was made available for Greek translation.

Though this omitted or falsified certain facts in the cause of trade security, the extant translation remains a gem of exploration literature. Significantly, the opening passage, proclaiming the aim of the enterprise, makes no mention of the gold market. 'The Carthaginians decreed that Hanno should sail beyond the Pillars of Hercules and found Libyphoenician colonies. He therefore set out with sixty ships, each of fifty oars, and with many men and women, about 30,000, with food and other necessities.'

If the number of emigrants were not an exaggeration, the sixty galleys must have accompanied transports, unmentioned in the report. After dealing briefly with the founding of the settlements, the narrative continues with an intriguing account of Hanno's explorations. The following is the text:

> *Having passed the Pillars and sailed on for two days, we founded the first colony, naming it Thymiaterium. By this lay a great plain. Sailing westward, we came next to a place called Soloeis, a thickly-wooded promontory. Here we built a sanctuary to the sea god* (Poseidon in the Greek text), *then sailed east for half a day until we reached a lagoon near the sea, filled with an abundance of tall reeds. Elephants were*

*feeding, and many other animals. For a day we skirted the
lagoon, leaving colonists at places named Fort Carion, Gytta,
Acra, Melita and Arambys. Next, we reached the Lixus, a
great river which flows out of the continent. On its banks
the Lixites, a wandering tribe, grazed their flocks. We stayed
with them for a period of days, becoming friends. Beyond
the Lixites dwelt Ethiopians* (black men), *inhospitable people
occupying a land of wild beasts divided by high mountains
from which, they say, emerges the river Lixus. In the region
of these mountains live men of strange appearance, the
Troglodytes. They could run faster than horses, so the Lixites
said. Recruiting interpreters from the Lixites, we coasted
south for two days beside uninhabited country, then east for
another day. We came now to a gulf containing a small
island, about five stades* (three quarters of a mile) *in circumference. We called it Cerne and placed a station on it. This
place we judged exactly opposite to Carthage, for the voyage
from Carthage to the Pillars equalled that from the Pillars
to Cerne. From here, encountering a great river which is
called the Chretes, we came to a lagoon containing three
islands, each larger than Cerne. A day's sailing brought us
to the far end of the lagoon, overshadowed by towering
mountains in which lived savages clad in the pelts of wild
animals. They stopped us landing by throwing stones at us.
After reaching another broad river, full of crocodiles and
hippopotami* ('river-horses'), *we returned to Cerne.*

*Later, we sailed south again from Cerne, following the
coast for twelve days. The whole land was inhabited by
Ethiopians who fled at our approach. Their tongue was in-
comprehensible, even by the Lixite interpreters. On the
twelfth day we drew near a range of high mountains covered
with aromatic trees of coloured wood. Sailing beside these
for two days, we came to a great bay with flat land on
either side. At intervals during the night, fires flared up in
all directions. Taking on water, we skirted the coast for five
more days until reaching an immense gulf which the interpreters called West Horn. In it was a big island, and within*

the island a lagoon containing yet another island. Landing,
we saw nothing except forest, but at night fires burned and
we heard pipes, cymbals, drums and multitudinous shout-
ing.

Terrified, we departed swiftly, coasting a region scented
with the smell of burning wood. Streams of fire plunged to
the sea, and the heat prevented an approach to land. Con-
tinuing apprehensively and without delay for four days, we
saw nocturnal fires at the centre of which one blaze rose
above all others, appearing to touch the stars. This, it
transpired, was the highest mountain we had seen, and was
called the Chariot of the Gods.

On the third day of our departure from this place, having
sailed beside more fiery streams, we came to a gulf called
the Southern Horn. At the head of this gulf was an island
resembling the last mentioned in that it enclosed a lake
containing another island. This was full of savages, of whom
the greater number were women. Their bodies were covered
with hair, and the interpreters called them Gorillas. We
pursued them. The men were too elusive for us, climbing
precipices and throwing down rocks, but we caught three
women who bit and scratched their captors. We killed and
skinned them, bearing their pelts back to Carthage. We went
no further; our provisions were inadequate.

Beset with obscurities, deliberate or otherwise, the Hanno
report has fascinated and frustrated countless scholars. Their
interpolations form a subject in its own right. Briefly, expert
opinion, though divided in detail, has become decreasingly
sceptical as time has passed.

Among other ancients, Pliny the Elder was unimpressed by
Hanno's claims. On the basis of the report, he protested, many
fabulous things were asserted 'of which, in fact, neither
memory nor trace remain.' Later scholars found it difficult to
believe that the Carthaginians had outsailed medieval mariners.
Throughout the middle ages, it was noted, Arab sailors never
managed to progress beyond Cape Yubi, the southernmost

point of the Moroccan coast. Even the Portuguese did not succeed until the 16th century.

Two factors invalidate the objection that such an exploit was navigationally and logistically impossible. 1, the combination of winds and currents which baffled medieval sailing ships was not insuperable for galleys which could travel under oarpower. 2, long stretches of the Mauretanian coast, arid and lifeless in Christian times, were life-supporting in previous centuries. The dehydration of the Sahara, as mentioned, has accelerated rapidly. In Hanno's day, wadis now long dry bore fresh water to the western shore.

Modern commentators observe the matter-of-fact quality of the report and the absence of such fantasies as might be expected in fictional passages. Indeed, the descriptions of tropical exploration – the largely credible savages, the drums in the night, the bush fires, the timbers of the rain belt – bear an authenticity beyond the range of guesswork. Comparison with reports by European voyagers a thousand years later shows remarkable consistency.

When it comes to identifying specific locations there is more doubt. The vagueness, if not deceptiveness, of the navigational information is conspicuous, especially in relation to that area most vulnerable to rival penetration, the Moroccan coast. Of the colonies founded, only two can be placed with some assurance: Thymiaterion, on the river Sebou, and the island of Cerne (Herne) in the bay of the Rio de Oro, between Cape Bojador and Port Étienne.

There is also a striking omission. While mentioning a river Lixus south of 'Soloeis' (Cape Santin), Hanno gives no indication of Lixus itself, a commercial station already established beyond Tangier. Probably, his Lixite interpreters were not natives in the true sense but seasoned colonists. The Troglodytes, or cave-dwellers, are introduced on hearsay. Ancient writers apply the name to tribes in various parts of Africa, Herodotus adding to their alleged fleetness that their speech was like the screeching of owls.

From Cerne, the base for Hanno's explorations, two

southerly voyages are described. The first, and shorter, appears to have terminated at the delta of the Senegal, identified in the report as the 'Chretes' and the river of hippopotami and crocodiles. The second and more sensational reconnaissance seems to have taken the travellers beyond Cape Verde, the wooded range twelve days from Cerne, into regions strange even to the Lixites.

If modern exegesis is correct in recognizing 'West Horn' as Bissagos Bay, and the 'Chariot of the Gods' as Mount Kakulima, then the Carthaginians have a strong claim to have been the first civilized people to have explored the coasts of Portuguese Guinea and French Equatorial Africa.

True, Herodotus believed that Phoenician mariners had circumnavigated Africa in the 7th century, but the tale is enigmatical. Later, Xerxes of Persia promised, somewhat less than magnanimously, to pardon the condemned courtier Sataspes if he sailed round the continent. Sataspes indeed travelled south from Tangier beyond the Saharan fringe, but just where he turned back is unknown. In any case, he could hardly have got so far without Phoenician, probably Carthaginian, co-operation.

By comparison, the scale of Hanno's expedition was grandiose. The Atlantic coast was not merely navigated but stationed to a point near the tropics. According to extreme interpolation, the 'Chariot of the Gods' was the volcanic Mount Cameroon, carrying the exploration beyond Cape Palmas to the bight of Biafra, though this seems unlikely even ignoring the sailing times.

Finally, the closing reference to 'Gorillas' has raised dispute. The giant anthropoid apes were named, after Hanno's description, by their modern discoverers. Scholars are divided as to whether the report itself concerns apes or human beings, one school asserting that the captives were hairy Pigmies, another that they were apes, but specifically chimpanzees. At all events, the skins were a sufficient novelty in their day to be placed on public show at Carthage.

c*

*   *   *

While Hanno sailed south, other mariners turned north up the western coast of Europe to Brittany. Their quest was not for gold but tin, increasingly valuable to a developing Punic bronze industry. The inspiration came from Tarshish. The Tartessians traded with a Breton people, the Oestrymnians (in legend, of Spanish origin), knowing from them of Ireland and England. At Gades, Carthaginian merchants were well-placed to learn of such connections. They resolved to tap the northern trade.

Even less is known of Punic exploration in the dangerous waters of Biscay than of the southern expeditions. The lengths to which the pioneers would go to preserve their secrets are mentioned by Strabo, who cites the deliberate wrecking of vessels by captains who found themselves followed. Nevertheless, a brief description of northern conditions survives in the name of one Himilco, said by Pliny to have adventured 'at the same time' as Hanno.

It occurs in the writing of a much later Roman scholar and poet, Avienus, who referred to the Oestrymnians as inveterate traders, brave and energetic, with skin-covered ships in which they sailed 'the stormy channel.'

From their country to the sacred island, as it was known of old, takes two days sailing. The island covers a vast area and is inhabited by the Hibernian people. Nearby lies the island of Albion. Carthaginians, together with people living round the Pillars of Hercules and Tartessians, all visited these regions.

The Carthaginian Himilco, who describes how he tried this voyage, says that it takes at least four months. There is no wind to hasten the ship, and the lazy waters of the ocean seem asleep. From them rise shoals of seaweed which often restrain the ship like a thicket. Nevertheless, he says, the sea is not very deep. Aquatic creatures swim here and there, and sea-monsters pass between the becalmed ships.

Sluggish waters and lack of wind is not the impression expected from a sea voyage to the north of Spain, yet the chance of encountering a dead calm beyond the 45th parallel was not remote, and Himilco was generalizing from a single trip. As for sea-monsters and seaweed, whales were common at one time in the Bay of Biscay; ancient mariners spoke of algae far from the Sargasso (the large quantities washed up on the Channel Islands and the Breton coast were once used on the fields as fertilizer). If the sea appeared shallow to Himilco it was because the galleys hugged the gently-shelving bays and offshore sand-banks.

The extent of Carthaginian exploration in the north is problematical. There is no evidence that Himilco visited England or Ireland, but it would not be improbable. On the other hand, lack of Phoenician relics in the British isles, and of Punic settlement on the shores of Portugal and Galicia, suggests that the feasibility of importing tin directly from the north by sea was soon discounted. Despite intermediaries, the land routes were quicker and safer.

Regardless of trade results, Hanno and Himilco stand among the great explorers, the dilators of the known world. Other Carthaginians, now anonymous, doubtless deserved equal fame. Familiar with tides that bemused the Romans centuries afterwards, Punic seamen braved an ocean few of their contemporaries contemplated – none without shuddering.

11: *War Lessons*

For most of the 5th century, Carthage, preoccupied in Africa, remained aloof from the incessant feuds and revolutions which upset life in Sicily. Against Syracuse, the dominant tyranny in the east, a well-fortified Motya guarded Carthaginian interests in the west. Through the rest of the island, states of varying complexion struggled stubbornly, aristocracies and democracies, Ionians and Dorians, Siceliots and Sicels (the native Sicilians).

Mindful of the costly fiasco at Himera, Carthaginian society, intrinsically unwarlike, was content with a passive role so long as its buffer on the near end of Sicily was undisturbed. Few of the mercantile families which governed Carthage prized a military tradition. Accumulation of wealth was their business, not its dissipation on expensive wars.

Punic intervention when Sicilian affairs took a turn for the worse, placing Motya and the west in jeopardy, was reluctant, protracted diplomacy delaying armed initiative. The corollary, a marked impatience to recall and disband armies once they had been deployed successfully, precluded the strategic exploitation of victories.

Despite such militarily inhibiting tendencies, it had to be admitted that the affluence created by the system was itself a substantial asset when the sword was drawn. It bought the foreign troops whose services enabled Carthaginian life and business to proceed largely undisturbed at time of war. It bought valuable alliances. It bought disaffection in the forces of the enemy. Indeed, so far as Carthage was unlucky to emerge at last with less than outright dominance, her renewed struggle in Sicily was to provide succinct testimony to the power of finance in war.

As it happened, the Sicilian campaigns commencing at the

end of the 5th century and proceeding throughout the 4th, may be said to have covered a great deal of territory without much changing Carthage's position in the island. The *History* of Diodorus, himself a Sicilian, recounts battles, depredations, plunder and atrocities with depressing monotony. From one extremity of the land to the other, campaigns rage. Tyrants rise, cities fall, martial heroes and miscreants come and go.

And, after all, Syracuse holds the east; Carthage still holds her western ground.

What indeed changed as war trundled back and forth was the Punic outlook. Inevitably, Carthage acquired an overlay of Greek tastes. A hundred years and more of conflicts, truces shifting alliances, could hardly fail to impress the ways of the island on the countless soldiers and diplomats who commuted from Africa. Carthage also acquired military technique. Repeated fighting produced skilled officers, refined war procedures.

That a community of traders from the balmy gulf of Tunis would ultimately alarm the hardened militarists of Rome into seeking its destruction had much to do with lessons learned in the Sicilian wars of the 4th century. From her Phoenician background Carthage could draw two military assets: the skill of her seamen, and an expert knowledge of building and attacking fortifications. Siege warfare, dating back to the earliest city foundations of Mesopotamia, evinced cogently by the Assyrians, was very much an Asian skill.

In open warfare, as the Persians had learned to their cost against Greek infantry, eastern modes were less dependable. The so-called Sacred Band at the core of Carthage's motley armies achieved fame at first for its ornament. Clad in resplendent costume and armour, feasting on gold and silver plate, battles commemorated by precious rings on their fingers, the affluent merchants' sons who filled its ranks aroused the wonder of Greek writers.

But their fighting technique – at least in the early days – seems to have been obsolete. Accounts of numerous chariots transported from Carthage to Sicily suggest a concept of warfare outdated by Greek tactics. If initial successes were dramatic, they owed more to the expendability of innumerable hired troops than to any sophistication of Punic arms.

*   *   *

Briefly, the events which precipitated Carthaginian intervention in Sicily after so many years concerned the violent rivalry of two Siceliot states, Segesta and Selinus. Situated in the west of the island, close to Phoenician territory, both communities had been friendly with Carthage until military conflict between them jolted Selinus into alignment with the eastern power of Syracuse.

Fear that Syracuse might establish a hold in the far west, endangering the one feature of northern strategy Carthage deemed sacrosanct, gave weight to Segesta's urgent calls for Punic aid – the more so since the Segestans were willing to make their city a dependency of Carthage. All the same, there was no hasty action. Only when diplomatic approaches to Selinus and Syracuse proved unsuccessful were the Carthaginians persuaded to intervene with armed force.

The expedition was entrusted to the first Carthaginian of note to bear the name of Hannibal (Grace of Baal), the son of a Magonid called Gisco. Grandson of the Hamilcar who had died at Himera, Hannibal had a personal motive for revenge by war. Diodorus dubbed him 'a Greek-hater.'

Hannibal landed in western Sicily in 410. Accompanied by a modest advance force, mainly of Libyans, he put a stop to Selinuntine aggression but was unable to attack Selinus itself until his full army of nearly 50,000 troops had gathered. The delay in fielding his Spaniards and Africans – a year had passed before all were assembled – demonstrated a major problem of reliance on mercenaries. Selinus was now besieged with grim efficiency.

Raising wooden assault towers and wielding battering-rams equipped with metal heads, Hannibal's troops breached the walls and poured into the city, robbing, raping and slaying

indiscriminately. If this were a tragic concomitant of em-
ploying 'barbaric' troops (the Greeks attributed the worst to
the Iberians), their commander showed no remorse. Begged
to ransom the citizens who had escaped death, Hannibal re-
torted that those who could not defend their freedom must
try their hands at slavery. As for the temples, shamelessly
looted, the fall of the city was evidence, claimed the general,
that these had been deserted by the gods.

Joined by hordes of Sicels eager to witness Greek discom-
fiture, the victorious army next marched to avenge the humiliation of Himera. A small force of Syracusans had reinforced
the city, but the magnitude of the assault was overwhelming.
About half the population contrived to escape by sea; of the
rest, the women and children were seized as prizes by the
foreign troops. About 3,000 male prisoners were led to the
spot where Hamilcar had met his death and butchered, on
Hannibal's orders, as a sacrifice to his dead relative.

Having perpetrated this odious deed and razed Himera, the
Punic general abstemiously refrained from the further conquests his success might have warranted, returning promptly
to Carthage and loud applause. Laboriously recruited, his host
dispersed in quick time. When circumstances soon demanded
a new campaign, recruiting officers had to set out for foreign
parts once again.

Within a short time of its sack, Selinus had been occupied
by a Syracusan leader named Hermocrates as a base for raids
on Phoenician land. Amid mounting tension, both Carthage
and Syracuse sought Sicilian and Italian allies, and appealed to
Greece. Athens backed Carthage; Sparta, Syracuse. But the
great states of Hellas were too fiercely engaged in their own
fight to send material help west. Hannibal was commissioned
to lead a second expedition, this time with the overthrow of
Syracuse as its aim.

Disembarking in southwest Sicily, the Punic army secured
the region of Selinus then marched east toward Syracuse. The
first place of size on the route was Acragas, a prosperous trading city celebrated for its public buildings, the richness of its

arts, its general opulence. Shutting their gates on the advancing host, the Acragantines declined either to join Hannibal
or pledge their neutrality. Independence was a local trait. A
natural stronghold perched upon rocky slopes, Acragas inspired its residents with confidence.

The investment of the city is interesting for a number of
phenomena featuring persistently in the wars:

Pestilence. A danger commonly associated with the conditions of ancient and medieval field camps, epidemic was
perhaps the most crucial of Carthage's enemies in Sicily. Diodorus described the symptoms as dysentry, delirium, swelling
of the throat and body pustules – conceivably typhoid. Though
not as disastrous at Acragas as elsewhere, the disease killed
Hannibal early in the siege leaving his lieutenant, Himilco, in
command.

Corruption. While chronic inter-state and internecine
rivalries among the Siceliots advises caution in accepting
charges of treason and bribery too readily, the frequency with
which they are imputed against politicians and generals
suggests the adept use of Carthaginian wealth in subverting
the opposing cause.

In a bid by Syracuse to relieve Acragas, a powerful force
from the eastern city defeated a Carthaginian contingent a
short distance from the beleaguered walls. For a moment, the
town garrison had a chance to sally effectively against a shaken
enemy. The failure of the Acragantine captains to do so raised
accusations of bribery against them, and four were stoned to
death by impassioned compatriots.

Religious attitudes. Hannibal's claim at Selinus that his
victory indicated the abandonment of the city by its gods
was unexceptional logic in antiquity, certainly among ancient
generals. Divine commitment to martial causes was vital to
participants, who watched for signs of holy displeasure with
fearful eyes. At Acragas, a cemetery outside the city was used
to provide material for the siege until one of the tombs was
struck by lightning. Immediately, Himilco stopped the desecra-
tion and offered a sacrifice to the gods.

When disease among the troops intensified, it was actually deemed provident to build a temple in Carthage to honour Demeter and Persephone, Greek deities much favoured in Sicily and thought likely to have had a hand in the pestilence.

The fall of Acragas, finally abandoned by its citizens in December 406, brought a more tangible aspect of Greek creativity to Carthage. Before the vast amount of booty was shared within Himilco's army, the most valuable works of art were set aside for Africa, to be greatly admired by the Carthaginians. The new year promised even better prizes. To the east of Acragas lay Gela, poorly fortified, then Himilco's real objective, Syracuse.

12: *Dionysius*

THE fall of Acragas, producing furore at Syracuse, tossed power to a remarkable demagogue named Dionysius. He had begun his career as a clerk in a public office; he was to rule Syracuse for thirty-eight years, becoming not only the most powerful of Siceliots but a force in Greek Italy, indeed throughout the Greek world.

A former adherent of Hermocrates, Dionysius had distinguished himself in subordinate rank during the attempt to save Acragas, a campaign which brought recrimination on the Syracusan generals and enabled him to make his move. It was a classic bid for tyrannical authority, based on popular anxieties, exploitation of class resentment and the ruthless sacrifice of colleagues.

Simultaneously boasting humble roots and seeking rich support, Dionysius assured his election to the board of generals by fervent speeches against the discredited commanders. Then, encouraging fear of Carthaginian invasion, he accused his fellows on the new board of negligence, calling for an overall commander. Invested with supreme powers as a crisis measure, Dionysius never looked back.

At first, his position was precarious. Himilco had advanced on Gela at the end of the winter; only prompt reinforcement could save the town. Dionysius marched with a hastily assembled army of some 30,000 troops, including Italiots (Italian Greeks) and non-Syracusan Siceliots, accompanied along the coast by a protective fleet.

Ambitiously, he planned to attack Himilco's position west of Gela in a multiple operation, part amphibious, part by land. The syncronization of assaults proved too difficult for unsophisticated units which, approaching the foe in succession, were defeated in detail. Dionysius, in Gela when he learned that his tactics had misfired, withdrew toward Syracuse amid a stream of Gelan refugees.

Only the loyalty of his professional guards now spared him the fate that had served the generals after Acragas. Aristocratic units of his cavalry, reaching Syracuse before him, took control and denounced his dictatorship. But they underestimated his determination. Fighting his way into the city, Dionysius overpowered the dissidents. By conceding terms favourable to Carthage, he obtained Himilco's recognition of his government.

The Carthaginian returned to Africa in triumph. Apart from the original dominion in western Sicily, Carthage had gained Segesta, Selinus, Acragas, Gela, the remains of Himera and other places, as dependencies, securing the separation from Syracuse of every other state on the island. Never had her Sicilian empire been greater, her treasury richer in booty. Never had a western power imposed itself with such authority on Greek affairs.

But the price was not negligible. For a long time the virus from Acragas, carried back on the troopships, plagued Carthage with wholesale death. For Dionysius, her grim preoccupation meant a perfect chance to renege on the peace terms. Building a massive stronghold to house his hired guards at Syracuse, he was soon oppressing his Siceliot neighbours, subjugating their cities and territories.

Beset by epidemic, the mercantile families which governed Carthage faltered at spending wealth and effort to protect the non-aligned Greeks. Procrastination proved more costly. Inexorably, Dionysius consolidated his eastern power, filling cities with his hirelings, importing Italian troops, forcibly shifting populations he did not trust. In Syracuse, a puppet government gave formal approval to the tyrant's schemes.

By 402, he was preparing openly for major war. The bastions of Syracuse were strengthened, its navy enlarged by 200 ships. Craftsmen were imported to make armour and weapons. Four years later, his plans complete, Dionysius proclaimed Carthage the enemy of all Greeks and called for the liberation of Punic Sicily. It was a popular message. Deluded by the prospect of Dionysian 'freedom,' the Siceliots hailed the end of dependence on Carthage.

At the head of the largest army remembered in Sicily, Dionysius marched straight across the island to Motya. Everywhere in his path, Greek populations, recalling Hannibal's atrocities, turned on the Carthaginians in their midst, slaughtering, torturing. At Motya, an alarmed garrison destroyed its causeway, resolved on desperate resistance. Months would pass before Carthage, now recruiting, could bring relief.

Dionysius, versed in Punic siege techniques, did not intend to wait. Building a mole to replace the demolished causeway, the tyrant hoisted missile troops on wooden towers to drive the defenders from their parapets while his miners and batterers worked below. Diodorus described the furious street-fighting which ensued within the breached citadel as the Phoenicians, 'their hope of living abandoned,' sold their lives expensively. The community was massacred.

Motya's fall marked the high tide of success for Dionysius against Carthage. Winter, and the disbandment of much of his army, was followed by the belated landing of Himilco at Panormus. The flood of war receded east again. Pausing to restore the old Phoenician territories, Himilco matched the tyrant's lunge at Motya with an equally brilliant blow at Messana on the far extremity of Sicily.

When the Messanians marched out to oppose him, the Carthaginian general dispatched an amphibious assault-force by the straits to outflank them and capture their seaport. The city, bereft of troops, fell with scarcely a struggle. Its occupation was a masterstroke. Apart from gaining an admirable harbour, Himilco had blocked the path for Italian reinforcements to Dionysius, opened the possibility of recruiting them for himself, and brought the approach to Syracuse from Greece within range of his sea patrols.

After the brief orgy of anti-Punic sentiment, the Siceliot states which had defected from Carthage renewed allegiance with alacrity. Some Greeks, including the Segestans, had stayed loyal in defiance of Dionysius. Most, on sober reflection, can have had little doubt that the tyrant's ambitions were at least as acquisitive as those of the southern traders.

Himilco now marched south on Syracuse. His intention, in accord with ancient method, was to move his fleet down the coast with his army abreast of it on the shore, but an eruption of Mount Etna forced the latter to divert through the interior. Quick to take advantage, Dionysius thrust his own army and navy north to challenge the unaccompanied Carthaginian armada. Unfortunately for the despot, his admiral and brother, Leptines, advanced his best ships too quickly and was mauled by the Punic fleet.

While Himilco reunited his forces south of Etna, Dionysius withdrew to Syracuse. He was cornered. True, the walls of the city, immense in length and resilience, were virtually impregnable, but support for his regime within was diminishing, as its allies outside. Moreover, Himilco commanded sea and harbour.

Then, in the summer of 396, pestilence once more struck the Carthaginians. Wrote Diodorus:

The disease first affected the Libyan troops. For a while, they were tended and buried. But soon the infectiousness of the sick, and the number of corpses, prevented anyone approaching . . . some went mad and lost their memory, rampaging deliriously through the camp attacking everyone . . . Death occurred on the fifth or sixth day of the disease, amid such pain that those who had been killed in battle were thought fortunate.

With the prospect of contamination spreading to the Carthaginian contingent – thus, as before, to Carthage herself – , Himilco took the damaging step of leaving his mercenaries to their own ends, raising the siege of Syracuse and departing with his compatriots. Much of the abandoned army extricated itself by dispersal, or by joining Dionysius. Carthage was spared infection. But repercussions were unfavourable.

Disaffection shook the African dominions. Particularly

shocked by the fate of the Libyan mercenaries, a horde of rebels advanced as far as the walls of Carthage before the insurrection lost impetus and fizzled out. The Carthaginians
themselves were appalled by the setback. Himilco, accepting
blame as a token of divine wrath, killed himself by fasting.

For more than a decade, Carthage was reduced to her old
lines in western Sicily. Dionysius, however, was not content.
Constantly belligerent, finally he provoked a new war about
381. This time the Carthaginian expedition was led by
Himilco's former admiral, Mago. The campaigns, located partly
in Italy, are obscure, but it seems that Carthage now had allies
among the Italiots, who found Dionysius increasingly ob-
jectionable.

Two battles are recorded in Sicily, at Cabala in the west, and
at Cronium near Himera. The first resulted in defeat for Mago,
who was among the killed. The second was a greater defeat for
Dionysius, with the reputed loss of 14,000 Siceliots and his
brother Leptines. Still, the dictator yearned to rule all Sicily.
In 367, he went to war for the last time. The conflict ended
with his own death.

The demise of Dionysius (he is said to have expired after
over-indulging at a banquet) left Carthage once more to her
old sphere in Sicily : the thin western end of the island. It was
a prosaic conclusion to almost forty years of wrestling with
the tyrant, but not without cause for satisfaction.

In Dionysius, Carthage had fought one of the most formidable and warlike rulers of the century; she had fought entirely
overseas, with all the disadvantages that entailed; and she had
coped with epidemic at the same time. Toward the end of the
period, notably at Cronium, Punic forces had shown themselves equal to powerful hoplite formations in the open field –
an achievement the vaunted Persian armies could not claim.

For all its complications, Carthage's military system had
functioned in general effectively, especially if the saving in
Carthaginian lives was accounted. Above all, by her own
calculation, there had been business as usual.

13: *Exit Greek Warriors*

WITH increasing coherence in the years which followed Dionysius, world events conspired to raise Carthage to the heights which at last became her catafalque. Little more than a life-span after the tyrant's death, the Greeks would have failed in their last bid for western power; the fall of Tyre would have left Carthage sole champion of the Phoenician heritage; Punic supremacy in Mediterranean waters would be recognized.

For the first time, the greatest city of Africa would have clashed with the state that was destined to extinguish her.

It is frustrating that Carthage, historically mute, emerges from this era mainly through Greek notices, leaving the limelight to Hellenic actors while the Punic cast is diminished to a list of names: the Magos, the Hannos, the Himilcos. Of the public figures and political careers of Carthage at the period almost nothing can be ascertained.

Two exceptions in the second half of the 4th century were political misfits; aspiring autocrats in a mercantile oligarchy. Their singularity attracted comment. The first, Hanno, known enigmatically as 'the Great,' was outstandingly rich. But the largesse he lavished in his bid for power brought him no success. He was executed with most of his family.

The second, Bomilcar, may be noted later. His revolt fared as poorly as Hanno's, emphasizing the strength of the 'establishment.' Relative stability of government had much to do with Carthage's ability to hold her own against the western Greeks, whose internal affairs were seldom steadfast. Post-Dionysian Sicily illustrated the advantage in its clearest form.

At Syracuse, a bitter struggle to succeed the late regime led to anarchy. Similarly torn by inner conflict, her dependent cities fell to an assortment of adventurers whose petty tyrannies shattered all sense of Siceliot unity. The eagerness of these self-seeking despots for outside support in their constant feuds disposed the island to increasing manipulation from Africa. Peaceful exploitation of a splintered Sicily was work tailored for the Carthaginian temperament.

It was without enthusiasm, therefore, that Carthage viewed the arrival of a new and potentially cohesive Greek force. About 345, a group of Siceliot aristocrats implored Corinth, the mother city of Syracuse, to assist in ridding them of the despots. Corinth, past the meridian of her powers, could not spare an army, but sent a small command of picked troops under a fanatical tyrant-hater named Timoleon.

Timoleon possessed a rare blend of attributes: the astute and ruthless aggression needed to match that of his chosen enemies, and a material disinterest entirely at odds with their own greed. Within three years of reaching Sicily, he had cleared Syracuse of its tyrannical factions, replaced the dungeons of Dionysius with courts of justice, and moved against the surrounding despots.

The struggle was desperate. Limited in men and provisions, Timoleon fought as unscrupulously as his opponents. In 342, his resort to plundering Carthaginian dependencies to supply his troops finally convinced Carthage that the threat to her interests justified armed intervention. A year later, her army landed at Lilybaeum, near Motya, a strong contingent of the Sacred Band with the vanguard.

Timoleon, imperilled by sheer numbers, was blessed with luck. At the head of some 10,000 men, he encountered the larger Punic force in the process of crossing a swollen river, the Crimisos. The battle which ensued resounds in Greek legend with miracle and portent, strikingly analagous to the biblical Megiddo and the waters of Kishon.

The Sacred Band had crossed the Crimisos ahead of its mercenaries, the latter delayed on the far bank by a rising stream. The odds were now reversed, Timoleon's troops far outnumbering the Carthaginian vanguard. Encumbered on soggy ground by sumptuous armour and panoply, the Sacred Band fought bravely until overwhelmed.

Meanwhile, the mercenaries, attempting to ford the torrent to their relief, were either swept off their feet or arrived too exhausted to be much help. Drenched by the river and lashing rain, the Carthaginian army forsook the field, retreating in poor shape to Lilybaeum. According to Plutarch, the losses of the Sacred Band at Crimisos, 3,000 by his estimate, were the greatest ever sustained in battle by citizens from Carthage – an interesting indication of the generally low cost of her wars in terms of Carthaginian blood, especially since the figure is probably an inflated one.

Timoleon's expulsion of the tyrants, completed with brilliant verve, proved less to the detriment of Carthage than she expected. Unsympathetic to democracy, the Corinthian favoured a political system not unlike that existing at the African city : that is, aristocratic, or rather plutocratic, the basic qualification not birthright but affluence. To the extent that wealth meant commerce rather than speculative aggression, Carthage anticipated eased relations with the Siceliot states.

Timoleon died in 337. For twenty years and more there was relative peace in Sicily. Distantly, Alexander blazed east toward the Indus; in the west, an inferior but ambitious captain strove for power at Syracuse. Agathocles, appearing first as a soldier pledged to democracy, took the classic path via popular revolution to dictatorship. Soon, emulating Dionysius, the new tyrant led his forces west.

But Agathocles lacked support beyond Syracuse. Provoked by his blatant aggression in 311, a Carthaginian expedition was quickly joined in Sicily by a swarm of native and Siceliot allies, routing the tyrant's army on the river Himeras. The Punic commander, Hamilcar-son-of-Gisco, was a popular ambassador. One by one, the Greek cities of the island took his side against Agathocles.

At this point, rather than await the onslaught of Hamilcar and most of Sicily, the tyrant conceived an astounding stroke : a counter-invasion of Africa to divert the Carthaginian army before it could overwhelm Syracuse. It meant weakening his forces in the city, but Carthage and her Tunisian provinces were weaker in garrisons. Coastal attack was outside their experience. That the beleaguered Agathocles should venture so far seemed to Carthage unthinkable. He lacked even a strong fleet.

Indeed, when he actually landed it was widely believed that the entire Carthaginian expedition must have perished in some appalling catastrophe.

Agathocles, having packed all the troops he could spare in a few dozen vessels, and dodged the Punic navy, reached Africa at Cap Bon. Here, compounding the audacity, he promptly burnt his ships. Probably, he had too few men to leave a guard on them. At all events, his army was left no alternative, whatever its fears, but to advance with him. The going was encouraging.

'Barns were crammed with everything conducive to good living,' wrote Diodorus. 'Sheep and cattle grazed the plains, and there were pastures full of horses.'

Horses were important, for Agathocles had brought none with him. Now, with cavalry to support his hoplites, he set about the countryside around Carthage. If Carthaginian unpreparedness was his chief fortune, he lacked neither boldness nor energy. In the time before his enterprise at last collapsed, Agathocles enlisted several native tribes to his banner, captured by Greek account 200 'cities' (mostly villages, in fact, though he took Hadrumetum, Thapsus and Utica) and fought a number of successful engagements.

Carthage, with most of her troops away in Sicily, was left with untrained warriors. Apart from her early confusion, a crisis of military leadership helped the invader. The two generals designated to repulse Agathocles, Hanno and Bomilcar, were bitter enemies, or they might have scored an early victory. As it was, the first battle was handed somewhat tamely to the presumptuous Greek. Unable to agree on tactics, Hanno led the right wing of the Carthaginian force in a fierce attack; Bomilcar held back, anxious to preserve his troops.

The resulting death of Hanno and strategic withdrawal of Bomilcar left the latter with supreme command at Carthage –

and an ambition more pressing than the destruction of Agathocles. Projecting crisis on crisis, Bomilcar staged an armed
coup. Diodorus recalled the scene:

> *Having reviewed the soldiers in the New City* (the sub-
> urbs?), *a short distance from Old Carthage, Bomilcar dismissed
> the majority, keeping back those in the plot . . . then he
> proclaimed himself the government. His men were deployed
> through the streets in five units, killing and suppressing re-
> sistance. In the confusion, the Carthaginians first assumed
> the city had been betrayed* (to the invaders) *but, perceiving
> the truth, the young men banded together against Bomil-
> car . . . Many Carthaginians occupied the tall buildings
> which surrounded the main square, showering missiles on
> the rebels below. At last, with many losses, the rebels
> formed close ranks and forced their way under fire through
> the narrow streets back to the New City, where they took
> position on a hill. But Carthage was now in arms against
> them . . .*

Thus the coup failed. With the rebels pinned down, the
citizens offered them amnesty 'in view of the external dangers
to the city.' But Bomilcar himself was put to death. The response of the people to a grave and dangerous situation,
fraught with complexity, was notably resolute. Time would
show that it was not an untypical reaction.

Agathocles, having failed to capitalize the episode, maintained his campaign until his troops grew weary and mutinous,
when he fled Africa for the unbreached bulwarks of Syracuse.
It is doubtful if Carthage, with sea command and her massive
walls, had been directly imperilled by the Greek assault.
Nevertheless, her economic losses had been considerable.
Characteristically, she chose peace to the expense of pursuing
the destruction of Syracuse.

One Greek antagonist of stature remained in Punic history.
Pyrrhus, king of Epirus in northern Greece, was a relative by
marriage of Alexander, and a warrior of scarcely lower repute,

Hannibal Barca later rated them together among the world's greatest generals. The monarch's intention, to succeed in the west as Alexander had succeeded in the east, was not implausible. He possessed, at the outset, an army of 25,000, and expected to swell it with Italiots and Siceliots.

The scheme, as Plutarch told it, was to conquer Italy, proceed to seize Sicily –'then who would not go on to Africa and Carthage?'

But Pyrrus was born too late for such an enterprise. By now, Etruscan power had been superseded by that of the Romans, a force already of huge confidence, its dominions spreading far to the Italian south. Pyrrus won battles against them (280 and 279), but so rugged were the Romans, so costly the victories, that he abandoned the struggle and, in 278, sailed to Sicily.

He found the island once more infested with petty Siceliot despots; yearning for a second Timoleon. Hailed as a saviour by the Greeks, he carried all before him until Carthage dug her toes in at Lilybaeum. Built since the fall of Motya, the stronghold incorporated everything the Carthaginians knew about defensive works. Here, after a triumphant passage through the island, Pyrrus ran headlong into unyielding walls; here, prestige dented, he languished until the Siceliots grew tired of his demands for men, money and sacrifice. When the saviour resorted to extortion, they began to drift to the Carthage camp.

In 276, a chastened Pyrrus withdrew his force from Sicily. As a farewell gesture, the Punic fleet fell in with his transports and scattered them. So vanished the vision of Greek empire in the west.

14: *Bodies Politic*

BY the 3rd century B.C., Carthage was accepted by ancient authors as a member of the exclusive club they distinguished as civilized : a mainly Hellenic body in a world of 'barbarians.' Too opulent for some tastes, too exotic for others, the white city on the shore of the dark continent possessed the ultimate sesame in her constitution. Contemporary thought was much concerned with systems of government. Whatever her rivals held against Carthage, there was wide agreement that her system was excellent.

Eratosthenes had no doubt that it entitled her people to Greek esteem. Aristotle quoted a general opinion that 'in many respects it is superior to all others'– a judgement with which, on the whole, he was in accord. 'A State is well-ordered when the commons are steadily loyal to the constitution, when no civil conflict worth mentioning has occurred, and when no one has succeeded in forming a tyranny.' Less pleasing to the philosopher was the importance in Carthaginian government of great wealth.

Details are scanty, but Greek observers defined the constitution of Carthage as a mixture of three elements familiar in their own régimes : the aristocratic, represented in what can be termed the senate, or deliberative body; the democratic, represented in popular assemblies; and, at least during much of the city's development, some form of monarchical element.

Aristotle, writing in the 4th century, spoke of kings at Carthage. Hamilcar who died at Himera, Hanno the colonizer and explorer, and Himilco-son-of-Gisco, among others, were described in Greek accounts by the word *basileus*, or king. But they were not monarchs in a full sense. Indeed, they were compared expressly with the kings of Sparta, survivors of an older age whose powers had withered. As at Sparta, Carthaginian kings acted as generals in many wars. Unlike their Spartan counterparts, they were elected.

When historians turned to 3rd century Carthage, the term 'king' disappeared and heads of state were referred to as magistrates or sufets (a Roman corruption of the Hebrew *shophet* = judge). Elected annually, at least two in number, the Carthaginian sufets presided over the senate and controlled the civil administration as well as functioning in a judicial role.

According to Aristotle, officers of state were unpaid at Carthage. Men of wealth, they seem hardly to have grown poor in service. The lucrative opportunities open to the governing class, leading at length to its decadence, were reflected in the scandals denounced by Hannibal Barca. But, until grossly abused, the system flourished.

Affluent families, filling the 300-strong senate, exercised control over all public affairs, legislating, deciding on peace and war, providing an inner council which guided the sufets. The senate also nominated a panel of inquiry – the so-called court of a hundred judges – to which state officials, particularly generals, were accountable. An important check on the power of the military, this court was said by Justinus to have originated in the 5th century due to fear of the Magonid commanders.

> When the power of the house of Mago endangered public freedom, a court of a hundred judges was formed among the senators. Generals returning from war were obliged to account to the court for their actions so that, being kept in awe of the state's authority, they might bear themselves in military command with due regard to the laws of Carthage.

The device was effective. Though command of hired armies without deep loyalty to Carthage offered obvious temptation to generals with political ambition, only one, Bomilcar, is known to have used troops in an attempted coup. In fact, despite the harsh treatment of unsuccessful commanders –

some were exiled or even executed – Carthaginian generals showed notable devotion to the state, often through service of many years.

Senators held office for life, seemingly co-opting new members when places fell vacant. The consistency of the body and its performance was accordant with a self-renewing system capable of reconciling internal discord; a close-knit establishment bound by class interests and social codes. Livy indicated that political affairs at Carthage were debated at society meetings and banquets before formal resolution in the senate.

The powers of the popular assembly are uncertain. Probably, it ratified the election of sufets, provided a third opinion when senate and sufets (or kings) disagreed, and was lobbied to bolster support for risky ventures. While conditional on property ownership, membership of the popular assembly represented modest wealth against the riches of the senate. Opposition between the groups was recurrent, but not critical so long as most citizens prospered.

Aristotle noted that the oligarchy at Carthage allowed the masses a liberal share of profits. Among a people more attached to commerce than politics – moreover, spared the social upheavals of war service – there was much to be said for the status quo. In contrast to the Siceliots, the Carthaginians seem never to have supported an aspiring dictator in any numbers. It was to take a rare combination of economic distress and corruption to alter things.

*   *   *

Not the least part of Carthaginian solidarity was the city's spiritual character. Religious intensity, linked with a disposition to honour one god above others, made for unity. In the early period, the supreme male deity Baal Hammon, sometimes wrongly called Moloch (a sacrificed offering, not a god), held sway with formidable compulsion. Then came something of a revolution.

From the 5th century, a virgin goddess, Tanit, became the

centre of popular worship. Softer and more approachable than the awesome Baal, her appeal blossomed beside the orchards and fields of the newly acquired African territories. Though commonly associated with the Phoenician goddess Asherat (Astarte), Tanit may have owed her name, as well as something of her nature, to the Libyans.

There were other cults. Above a flock of minor deities (*alonim* and *baalim*) stood the Tyrian Melkart, identified by the Greeks with Hercules; Eshmoun, identified with Aesculapius the healer; and a sea-god associated with Poseidon, or Neptune. Also connected with seafaring was Patechus, or Pygmaeus, a grotesque monster like the Egyptian Ptah, whose image was placed on the prows of ships to frighten enemies.

Despite vocational priests and priestesses, and probably priestly schools, the supervision of religious matters in Carthage was entrusted to a council of ten senators. The merchant families of the governing class were too practical, it seems, to allow the growth of a despotic priesthood.

The outside praise bestowed on the constitution of Carthage did not extend to her religious observances, which the Greeks and Romans condemned for embracing human sacrifice. Though largely replaced by animal sacrifice in the later centuries, there is no doubt that the practice occurred on a large scale later at Carthage than in Greece or Roman Italy. Diodorus described the sacrifice of 500 children from leading families at the end of the 4th century.

That such holocausts actually took place was put beyond doubt by the modern discovery in the Sanctuary of Tanit of thousands of urns containing the charred bones of children. Tophets with similar urns witnessed sacrifices at Hadrumetum, Motya, Sulcis, and other Phoenician foundations. Centuries after the Canaanites had felt obliged to offer 'first-fruits' to their gods, their descendants could still believe that the success of Agathocles in Africa was divine punishment for their avoidance of sacrifice.

At the same time, it should be said that Greek and Roman denunciations, inspired as much by political hostility as moral fervour, strike a note of hypocrisy. The Greeks left more children to perish of exposure and starvation than the Carthaginians burnt, while the Roman taste for slaughter, eventually indulged for sheer pleasure, scarcely needs comment.

Nevertheless, the topic raises a distinction in racial psyche.

The only mortals the Carthaginians accorded divine status were those, such as Dido, who destroyed themselves. Not surprisingly, a people who considered mystic suicide the most deserving of all acts was prepared on occasion to sacrifice themselves, or their own, for the national good. Their moral code is a lost book. Yet, while love and compassion are universal, these seem not to have received the higher endorsement of religion at Carthage.

The concept of an ethically demanding divinity never illuminated worship there. The sins of which the Carthaginians accused themselves were ritual, not moral ones; the response expiatory rather than renunciatory. Thus, the gods remained, on the whole, an oppressive force.

Remarkably, considering the martyrological element in the society, its people appear to have attached little importance to the notion of an afterlife. Existence was earthbound; self-sacrifice consoled wholly by devotion to the state itself.

D

15: *Carthaginians*

To the east, the establishment of the great dynasties which emerged when Alexander died – the Antigonids, Seleucids and Ptolemies – , brought a period of stability in which Carthaginian commerce spread quickly to the Aegean and Nile ports. Imposing Phoenician money and measures on his empire, the first Macedonian king of Egypt, Ptolemy-son-of-Lagos, provided a strong inducement to Punic trade.

Hitherto, Carthaginian coinage, minted specifically to pay mercenaries, had conformed to Greek standards. Now, switching to the Phoenician standard, Carthage adopted money for general use, availing herself of the experience and good offices of Egyptian financiers, the most expert in the ancient world. Increasingly, Punic merchantmen plied the eastern Mediterranean.

Carthaginians were everywhere. Inscriptions record their presence at Athens and Delos. They did business at Thebes. They carved their names in the sepulchre of sacred bulls at Memphis. As the foremost brokers and carriers of the day, they served clients as diverse as their commodities.

Apart from corn from the African granaries and metals from Iberia, Carthage dealt in resin from Lipara and other islands off the toe of Italy; sulphur from Acragas (collected in the region of Etna); wax, honey and slaves from Corsica; cattle from the Balearics; wine from many shores to suit many tastes; dyes, perfumes, dates, animal skins, and so on. In Europe, as in Africa, trade was established not only with coastal populations but with inland communities.

Thus, the scope and complexity of Carthaginian experience mounted. To oriental traditions, African environment and Greek influence were added the impressions of citizens who had explored the Niger, crossed the Sahara, felt the swell of

Biscay, sailed the Nile, engaged in business from the English Channel to the Dardanelles. What had they become, these inveterate travellers, since Dido first landed in Africa? How did they appear to others in the years that remained of Punic history?

In many respects they still displayed their eastern origin, a source of unease among their western neighbours, whose suspicions at length gave teeth to Cato's prejudice. Wrote Plutarch: 'The Carthaginians are hard and gloomy, submissive to their rulers and hard on their subjects, cowardly in fear, cruel in anger, stubborn in decision and austere, caring little for amusement or life's graces.'

But Plutarch, born too late to know the people of whom he wrote, merely echoed the aversion of a bygone age. His charge of cowardice, palpably unjustified, casts doubt on the rest of his summary. Austere and gloomy? There is a note of melancholia in Punic fatalism, as in the nature of most passionate peoples. Yet Plautus, writing while Carthage was still alive, portrayed the Carthaginian Hanno as a colourful, by no means depressing rogue.

Nor did the showy trappings of the Sacred Guard, the gold drinking cups of its warriors, reflect austerity. It was certainly true that the Carthaginians were not besotted by lives of idle luxury. Rich merchants turned a hand, it seems, on the farms they bought with their profits, and were not afraid of hazardous voyages. Neither theatres nor public games were known at Carthage. But if the hard-headed merchants who ran the city placed a lower value on the arts than their competitors, they were not blind to fine craftsmanship.

Greek artisans lived and worked at Carthage, whose wealthier homes were embellished with Hellenic vases, lamps, mosaics, bronze and ivory statuettes, even bathroom suites identical to those found in Greece.

Carthaginian craftsmen, catering for the masses, and for the backward people of other lands who received their cruder artefacts in exchange for valuables, admittedly were inferior in technique and artistry to the Greeks. That the aesthetic standards of much at Carthage grated on the Greeks and Romans is without doubt. On the other hand, the portrayal of gods with dulcimers and zithers, and their association with various forms of dancing, suggests a chord with which the critics might have harmonized.

They might also have felt at home among the ample feasts and banquets staged by the wealthy to win political support or entertain friends. Though Plautus poked fun at African 'porridge eaters,' and Plato asserted that alcohol was widely forbidden in Carthage (including, he believed, before sexual intercourse), Punic cooks were in fact renowned for the excellence of their sweet and spiced dishes; wines a favourite drink. A Carthaginian recipe has survived for a type of local sherry the Romans knew as *passum*.

Cato's brooding scrutiny of the metropolis would have been returned by citizens of varying appearance. The city was a melting pot, its relics revealing skeletal similarity in some instances with remains at Tyre (perhaps true Phoenicians) but a predominance in the main of African, not excluding Negro, blood.

The somewhat slender frames of the skeletons, considered with the known physical endurance of the populace, hint at a wiry people of strong constitution, traits possessed by the Barbary nomads. Unlike many orientals in urban societies, the Carthaginian merchant class seems to have avoided becoming soft – perhaps thanks to its close connections with seafaring and agriculture, and the admixture of Libyan stock.

At the same time, the cult of physique never appealed to the society. While the Greeks admired the naked bodies of strong youths and lithe girls, the Carthaginians preserved an oriental disdain for such exhibition, wearing long clothes and seldom appearing even bare-headed. The traditional male garb was a straight, ankle-length robe, worn loose in the fashion of the Egyptian *galabieh*.

'Hey, you without a belt!' the Carthaginian was hailed in the *Poenulus*, his Greek accoster inquiring if he was wearing his bathrobe. Actually, though a source of amusement to the foreigner, the costume was a useful protection against heat and dust-storms.

Most Carthaginian men grew beards and covered their hair, often tightly curled, with a conical hat resembling the Muslim fez, or *tarboosh*. They also kept off the sun with a cloth, secured round the skull, which fell to the shoulders like a modern Arab headdress.

Female costume was closer to the Greek style. From an early period, Carthaginian women wore embroidered robes resembling those favoured by Ionian matrons, simple garments gathered at the waist and with a decorative band (the Greek *paryphe*) rising vertically from the hem. Feminine hair-styles kept pace with Hellenic trends. The tresses, invariably grown long, were variously straight or curled, pulled back or fringed, and worn with headband or chignon. At one period, coils over the ears were fashionable.

Both sexes wore perfume, seemingly liberally, and earrings. They were also tattooed. Carthaginian fondness for ostentatious jewelry offended Greek taste. Those who could afford it smothered themselves in expensive ornaments. Intricate pendants hung from the ears; throats were adorned with necklaces of turquoise, jacinth and gold; women of no particular distinction wore diadems.

Often, jewelry incorporated such astral symbols as crescents and pointed stars, or represented sacred animals, including snakes. Finger-rings were commonplace, at an early period containing seals of jasper or cornelian; later, intaglios. Both sexes sported bracelets, in addition to which the women wore massive anklets as familiar in Bedouin society.

If much of this was strange to European cultures, Punic manners were equally alien. Carthaginian courtesy, orientally demonstrative, was mistaken by Greeks and Romans for obsequiousness, a quality they despised. The Africans saw no indignity in prostrating themselves and kissing the feet of those they honoured. To the Roman, such behaviour was cringing servility, the more perplexing since its perpetrators were just as capable of fiery passion.

Sensual by nature, the Carthaginians observed social restraints of some sobriety. Wanton resort to carnal pleasure was strictly curbed. Monogamy was the general rule in sex relationships, husbands and wives not uncommonly being buried beside each other at life's end. No evidence exists of harims or extensive concubinage. Indeed, the status of women, at least among the upper class, discouraged male licence. Many possessed considerable political influence. Others, as priestesses, exercised direct authority over men.

Apart from the abnormal circumstance of child sacrifice, the Carthaginians appear to have cherished their offspring no less than did other people. There was a goddess (Vininam) to watch over infants, and one of the most remarkable relics found of the city was a set of doll's crockery: tiny cups, plates, jugs, jars and clay lamps.

So far as can be told, Punic education was largely practical. The emperor Julian said that Carthaginian children were apprenticed to the world at an early age, encouraged to work diligently and live a blameless life. Found among commercial families throughout history, this approach to the building of initiative and character is consistent with the prospects open to youths in Carthaginian trade.

All the same, formal tutorship certainly existed, and not entirely theological. Hannibal Barca was said to have studied strategy in text-books; the ladylike Sophonisba allegedly was accomplished in the humanities; one Hasdrubal, also known by the Greek name Cleitomachus, became head of the Academy at Athens. In the last century of Carthage there was a school of later Pythagoreans in the city, which also possessed libraries, probably of Greek as well as Carthaginian works.

The only Punic books now known are the writings of the agriculturist, Mago. Since they contained, among much else, veterinary prescriptions, probably there was a medical literature at Carthage. The presence of doctors is attested by inscriptions. At summer's height, when the marshes of the nearby lake stank like rotten eggs, disease was a serious problem in Carthage, as in Tunis through history. Against trachoma and many other infirmities hailed by the sirocco, the people appealed not only to medicine but the healing gods Eshmoun and Shadrapa.

Shadrapa's assistance was invoked also in cases of poisoning by the snakes and scorpions of the region.

Environmentally and culturally, Carthage was very different, in spite of Greek overtones, from the Roman state which now confronted her. In a city whose every nuance indicated social dissimilarity and competitive dynamism, a more adaptable foreigner than Cato might have felt apprehensive.

BOOK TWO

16: *The Fatal Enemy*

WATCHING the Tunisian farmer hoeing the dry soil on the prosaic site that today marks the home of ancient Carthage, it seems incredible that marbled temples, pillars of porphyry, great halls of state once towered on that spot within the mightiest battlements of Africa. Not even Cato can have imagined the complete and utter oblivion that was to befall the city following his fiat – an extinction so complete that the exact location of the metropolis, the heart of the Punic empire, was rediscovered with certainty only last century.

The fate of Carthage was finally sealed in 149 B.C. By then her forces, restricted by treaty after Zama, had been shattered by Masinissa of Numidia. Everything favoured a Roman intervention in Africa. Those, such as Scipio Nasica, who opposed the policy had lost ground. An immense Italian army was available: 80,000 infantry and 4,000 cavalry. Young men who had painstakingly dodged service in Spain now flocked to join an expedition which promised the spoils of the richest city in the world for slight effort. With them assembled shady dealers and camp followers of every kind.

The destination of the army was not revealed, but few, least of all the Carthaginians, had any doubt. In a hopeless position from which to negotiate, the Punic government prepared to buy peace at almost any price. Popular leaders held responsible for the Numidian war were condemned, among them the defeated general Hasdrubal, and the pro-Roman faction gained prominence.

But attempts at *rapprochement* were frustrated by the Romans. Carthaginian diplomats, seeking the terms on which the affray with Masinissa might be pardoned, were kept on tenterhooks with obscure allusions and veiled threats. The ancient historians put it simply. Asked repeatedly how Carthage might make amends, Rome replied that she wanted only 'satisfaction.' Asked what 'satisfaction' meant, the Romans rejoined that the Carthaginians knew that best themselves.

The technique, diplomatic war waged by confusion, produced a bonus for its exponents. While Carthage grew increasingly desperate to avert invasion, her western neighbour, Utica, lost nerve altogether and placed herself at Rome's disposal.

Assured a safe port of disembarcation in Africa, the Roman expeditionary force advanced to Sicily, increasing pressure on the Punic government. At this point, its members abandoned hope of buying peace through an indemnity or territorial bargain and, like Utica, offered a formal submission (deditio in fidem). Technically, the deditio gave Rome possession of all lands, cities and towns of the Carthaginians, who then held their freedom and way of life by concession rather than sovereign right.

On this legality, Rome justified the course upon which she was already set. The stock-in-trade of governments does not change. Among several unpleasant aspects of politics familiar to the modern world, the ancients knew all about cold war, class war, trade war, terrorism, martial coups, purges, assassinations, the so-called liberation of peoples and a dozen forms of legal and diplomatic bad faith. But it would be hard to find a more striking example of cynical deception by the leaders of a great state than that now employed by Rome to achieve her ends.

Five Carthaginian ambassadors arranged the deditio, a gesture their Italian hosts at last applauded as a wise move. Carthage, the Romans pledged, would be assured in return 'her territory, her sacred rites, her tombs, her liberty and her possessions.' The precise words are from Diodorus Siculus. The Carthaginians, for their part, were to provide 300 hostages from senatorial families, and await further instructions from the consuls in charge of the expeditionary army. This would be moved from Sicily and stationed at Utica.

In the guise of protector, therefore – but with a legal claim to more deadly powers – Rome had secured the crossing and landing of her armada from all opposition. It was left to the consuls to complete a game of ruthless calculation. They were two: M. Manilius and L. Marcus Censorinus. At Utica they staged a massive display of military power for envoys from Carthage, but their tactics were still diplomatic. With Rome's protection, they claimed, the Carthaginians had no need of their own arms and ought to surrender them.

To the remonstrances of the envoys, Censorinus (the more eloquent of the consuls, so Appian pictured him) replied that if the Carthaginians sincerely desired peace they would comply. 'Come now, hand over your weapons, public and private, and your war machines.'

Whatever its suspicions, the Punic government had yielded too much to change its acquiescent policy at this stage. Ancient report quantified the material surrendered as 200,000 sets of arms and 2,000 catapults, together with countless spears and javelins. The figures, disproportionate to Carthaginian troop strengths at any time, let alone since Zama, may at least be taken as a sign that the Roman invigilators were thorough.

Censorinus summoned the Punic representatives to Utica once more, this time for the *denoument*. Perhaps fearful of the outcome, Carthage sent a delegation of unusual size, including senators, priests and leading businessmen. Its aim, according to Appian, was to impress the consuls by its importance, but the Romans were unmoved. Civic pomp was no substitute for weaponry; disarmed, Carthage lacked convincing argument. Her envoys listened in stunned silence as Censorinus disclosed his orders to destroy the metropolis.

> *Accept with courage the final command of Rome. Surrender Carthage to us and withdraw into your territory, remaining at least ten miles from the coast. We intend to raze your city to the ground.*

Casuistically, it could be claimed that such instructions were not inconsistent with Rome's earlier assurances, which apparently failed to specify the fate of the city as distinct from that of its occupants. Explaining the order for inland settlement, Censorinus pointed to the maritime element in Punic history. 'When you look at the sea you recall great fleets, their spoils, your docklands and arsenals.' The Carthaginians, he concluded, must forget their imperial past and consider a new, pastoral existence.

It was, as everyone understood, a bleak prospect. Large urban communities cannot be transposed to open country and survive intact. Denied ships, wharves, workshops and protective battlements, the mass of Carthaginians would either starve to death or become the defenceless prey of tribal warriors. As much was indicated by the outburst of protest with which the embassy responded when the full extent of Roman perfidy was evident.

Bitterly, its members reminded the consuls of Carthaginian compliance with the treaty agreed after Zama, of the punctilious payment of the indemnity and of the city's wholly accommodating approach to Rome since the war with Numidia. Solemnly, one speaker, Banno, urged the Romans to consider the reputation of their own state and to reflect on the ultimate judgement of history.

His appeal was discounted. All protests unavailing, the Carthaginian representatives weighed their own position. Some, deeply implicated in the policies which had led to the present pass, sought refuge with the consuls, or fled for foreign sanctuaries, fearful of the wrath of their compatriots.

The rest returned grimly to Carthage, passing tight-lipped through a city already inflamed by rumour. Accounts of what followed vividly illustrate the trauma of a great commercial state confronted with the vision of imminent extinction. In the senate, members listened horrified to the news of the returned ambassadors, interrupting with cries of profound dismay. These, confirming the worst fears of the crowds outside, provoked a political reaction of the most violent character.

At a stroke, the government was swept aside in an eruption of despairing anger described by Appian as orgiastic. Pro-

Roman senators and others of the appeasement faction were torn to pieces or stoned to death. Italians found in the city were hounded and massacred. Gods were abused. Mothers whose children had been given as hostages besieged the authorities, dementedly venting grief and recriminations.

Born of impassioned hatred for the faithless enemy, a new government of popular resistance arose from the bloodbath. Hastening to the city armouries, its supporters found nothing but empty stands. Equally desolate were the great horse-shoe stalls in the triple walls, once occupied by squadrons of elephants. At the naval docks, long-standing reserves of timber testified to the absence of naval construction in accordance with the treaty of 201.

If the Romans were to be opposed, it seemed likely that few Carthaginians could depend on more than their bare hands.

But if any paused in their fury to contemplate the outcome, a defence, however desperate, must have appealed to the passionate Punic temperament as a better end than abject deprivation in exile. Ten miles away, the bristling cohorts of Censorinus and Manilius eagerly awaited their destructive task, and the loot involved. Contemptuously, Carthage slammed her gates and declared herself at war with Rome.

17: *Came the Crow*

THE springs of Catoist bitterness toward Carthage, and the exceptional ruthlessness employed in disarming her, could be traced to the Sicily vacated by Pyrrhus. In legend, the Greek looked back at the island as his fleet withdrew and sighed prophetically: 'What a beautiful battlefield we leave to Rome and Carthage!'

Until then, the history of Romano-Punic relations had been pacific, even co-operative. In the beginning, Carthage, the richer and greater power, had regarded the Romans, like the Etruscans (whose kings indeed governed Rome in the 6th century), as a northern check to Greek ambitions in the west. When Rome, shaking off Etruscan dominance, established her republic in 509, a treaty with Carthage regulated their respective spheres. By this agreement the Romans would not sail west of Carthage, and undertook to trade elsewhere in Africa and in Sardinia only under the supervision of the Punic authorities. The Carthaginians pledged in return to respect Roman interests in the Latin towns and not to pursue colonial ambitions in Latium.

The ability of Carthage to impose sweeping trade restrictions was even more emphatic in a further treaty, signed in 348, now excluding Roman merchants from the whole of North Africa, as well as from Sardinia and southern Spain. Soon afterwards, Rome, incorporating most of Campania in her confederacy, was plunged into bitter conflict with the neighbouring Samnites. While the Latin power was preoccupied securing and expanding her Italian territories, Carthage continued to advance her mercantile dominance. In 306, a third agreement consolidated her trade monopolies.

The arrival of Pyrrhus in the 3rd century drew the two states together in common cause. While Roman manpower bled the Greek king of the strength to sustain his bid in

Sicily, Carthage promised silver to help finance Rome's resistance, and ships to offset her lack of sea power. Eliminating the Greek challenge, the combination left western supremacy disputable between its components.

Within a few years of the departure of Pyrrhus, his fabled prediction was historic fact.

Responsibility for the long and costly conflict known as the First Punic War is debateable. Philinus of Agrigentum, a pro-Carthaginian historian of the time, held the Romans to blame for crossing troops to Sicily in contravention of a treaty forbidding such a movement. Polybius, writing later, denied that the Romans were in breach of faith. At least it may be agreed that, sooner or later, a clash was inevitable.

Hitherto ranked by the Greeks as barbarians, the Romans had emerged from the widely reported onslaught of Pyrrhus with new status and confidence. From now on there could be no doubt that Rome was a major power. From as far as Egypt, envoys hastened to propose pacts. Stable in government, experienced in warfare, with large reserves of disciplined manpower, she could hardly fail to disturb the equanimity of rival states.

Economically, Carthage was a rival whose jealously protected advantages were bound to prick Rome. With naval dominance, the Punic power might have felt complacent were it not for the stepping-stone of Sicily, the logical extension of Italian empire for a state without a sea force. The short hop across the straits could be made by using ferry boats. In short, the temptation for Rome to stake an interest in the island was dangerously at odds with Carthage's long-held strategic view of Sicily.

Ostensibly, the war arose from an incident. For some time Messana had been occupied by Campanian mercenaries, the Mamertines (after Mamers, the Oscan Mars), who had come to Sicily originally to serve Agathocles. Settled on the straits, the piratical Mamertines were such a nuisance to the people of Syracuse that, about 265, the new ruler of that city, Hiero II, decided to drive them from the island.

The Mamertines, steadfast opponents of Pyrrhus in former days, sought help from his other ex-enemies. Both Rome and Carthage responded with units to reinforce Messana's garrison. When, in circumstances now uncertain, the Carthaginian commander was induced to withdraw in favour of the Roman guard, the scene was set for 'escalation'.

Roman troops were in Messana. To eject them, Carthage joined forces with Hiero. It was an unnatural alliance, conceived without enthusiasm, and short-lived. Syracuse had lost her former power; Carthage had had no time to raise her mercenaries. So far, operations were on a restricted scale. Then, in 264, the Romans crossed reinforcements to Messana on a fleet of rafts, raised the siege imposed by Hiero and marched on Syracuse.

Hiero now had second thoughts. A number of Sicilian cities, always ready to profit from upsets, had already made cause with the Italians. Hiero took the same step, contracting an alliance with Rome that was to endure for the rest of his long life. It was a prudent move, placing him with Masinissa among the few foreign kings to perceive the huge potential strength of the Roman state.

His defection, giving Rome control of the east coast and encouraging other Siceliots to make terms with her, left Carthage no option but to mobilize in full force. The war that ensued was to span a generation, produce the heaviest casualties then known to history and lead to radical strategic innovation on both sides.

Never before had Carthage's dependence on a hired army been tested against an enemy with so vast a reserve of fighting men and such efficiency of mobilization. Embarrassed by the usual delays in mustering, the Carthaginians were compelled to adopt a defensive role in their Sicilian strongholds (Acragas, Lilybaeum, Panormus and elsewhere) until their mercenaries were organized.

Rome, on the other hand, was impeded by the lack of a navy and maritime tradition. So long as Carthage's fleets were unchallenged, the well-fortified Punic ports in Sicily could withstand indefinite siege by land, their provisions assured by sea. At the same time, the Italian coast was vulnerable to naval raids. At last, Rome was under pressure to build a fleet.

Meanwhile, her operations centred on Acragas, an easterly Punic base which, being inland, could be sealed off by Roman troops. In 262, four legions were deployed in the investment. Five months brought the city near starvation, then the full mercenary army of Carthage arrived in Sicily. Including Iberians, Celts and Ligurians, its strength is uncertain, but events suggest it was fairly well matched against the Romans at Acragas. Neither its commander, Hanno, nor the consuls besieging the city, were eager to give battle.

Indeed, the opposed armies faced each other inactively for fully two months while conditions in Acragas deteriorated and the siege force itself, cut off from supplies by Hanno, suffered. Finally, signals from the garrison notifying the critical plight of the citizens prompted the Punic general to action.

Tactically, Acragas was a Roman victory. Hanno retired from a day-long battle in moderate order but undoubtedly the loser. Strategically, the outcome was more complex. For one thing, the engagement enabled the garrison of Acragas to evacuate without loss. For another, the Roman commanders (L. Postumius Megellus and Q. Mamilius Vitulus) committed a resounding error in sacking the city and enslaving its Siceliot occupants.

A great deal rested on the sympathies of the Siceliot communities, a number of which had already given valuable help to the Romans. Now the mood changed. Widespread anger at the treatment of the Acragans did much to consolidate support in the island for Carthage. Far from exploiting the victory over Hanno, the Romans lost ground, on balance, during 261. It was, however, an auspicious year for them in one field. The date marks Rome's decision to build a fleet. So far, the few ships she possessed had largely been provided and manned by Italiots, the *socii navales* or 'naval allies.' Resolved at last to take to the water, the 'landlubbers' displayed their practical nature in a telling light.

Their models, Greek and Punic, included (according to Polybius) a Carthaginian quinquereme or five-banked vessel wrecked on the coast of southern Italy. But the finer graces of such elegant craft were not for a people who frankly admitted their limitations as sailors. The 120 warships which comprised the first production order were of a species the precise likeness of which had never been seen before.

Heavier and slower than the sleek galleys of Carthage – as befitted a race which liked its feet on a solid base – these ponderous barges were peculiar for the extraordinary superstructure on their foredecks. Holding no hope of matching the seamanship of an enemy whose customary ramming and oar-smashing techniques demanded skilful manoeuvres, the Romans had resolved to make sea-fighting as much like land warfare as possible. To this end, they had equipped their ships with draw-bridges by which the legionaries on board could charge the crews of hostile vessels.

These bridges, four feet wide and twenty-four feet in effective length, pivotted on the base of a special foremast which supported the operating mechanism: an unwieldly boom and pulley system connected by rope with the far end of the boarding-bridge. Beneath this protruded a sharp spike to engage the deck of the enemy.

From its metal beak and violent pecking action as it dropped, the contraption came to be known as a *corvus* (crow). In battle, the crows were dropped hopefully on any hostile deck which came in range until the spike engaged. Then, protected by their shields, the Roman marines would storm the grappled enemy.

The first test of the new Roman navy was a fiasco. An advance force of 17 ships sent to the Sicilian theatre was challenged by 20 Carthaginian vessels among the Lipari islands. Here, the raw crews, recruited from elements of the *proletarii* considered undesirable by land commanders, promptly deserted and the squadron surrendered without a blow.

But if the Punic seamen derided the unsightly craft of their novice opponents, they were soon to learn a lesson familiar in the annals of warfare: namely, that relatively crude improvisation can achieve surprising objectives if confidently handled.

When the main Roman fleet appeared off northern Sicily, the commander of the Carthaginian naval forces there, a little-known Hannibal, unwisely approached without caution. The navies met off Mylae, not far from Messana. Hannibal, outnumbered in ships by the cumbersome enemy with their curious superstructures, nevertheless engaged with sanguine assurance, neglecting proper battle order.

The Romans, now with disciplined crews, were in two lines under the consul Caius Duilius; in all, 143 ships. As the swift Carthaginian vessels swung at them, aiming to rip oars and steering paddles from bulky hulls, the Romans manned their booms, the spiked crows poised in readiness. Unsuspectingly, the Punic pack bore in on the first line of the enemy. Violently, the boarding-bridges smashed down. The metal beaks rammed home.

Desperately, the rearward Carthaginian ships veered aside as heavily-armed legionaries poured aboard the grappled leaders. Some of Hannibal's galleys, slipping through the first Roman line, ran foul of the stabbing crows of the second line. Pierced and wallowing, they too were overrun by the 80 or so marines on each Roman ship. By the time the startled Carthaginians broke away, 45 of their craft were lost, mostly captured.

Mylae, celebrated in Rome by a triumphal column incorporating the figure-heads of the conquered vessels, marked the end of Punic naval dominance. Carthaginian seamen were still superior in professional skills, and would modify their tactics to meet the enemy, but Rome had shown she could live in their element, and quickly enlarged her fleet.

Four years after Mylae, it outnumbered the Carthaginian navy and was ready for the most ambitious foreign enterprise yet entertained by Rome.

Like Agathocles, the Romans intended to attack Carthage in Africa. Their early successes in Sicily had not brought the further gains expected. The cost of war there was heavy.

Unlike Agathocles, however, they diverted in no sense of desperation. The Africa enterprise was long planned, the resources applied to it massive. In the year 256, an armada of 350 vessels, the transports packed with supplies and horses, the warships jammed with legionaries and equipped with crows, sailed from Econmus in Sicily for the southern continent.

18: *Xanthippus*

A century later, under the passport of diplomatic deception, Roman troops would cross to Africa with impunity. In 256 the passage was formidable. Unenamoured of the open sea, the invaders planned to sail the southern coast of Sicily to its western extremity, where the traverse to the shores of Tunisia was shortest. This meant skirting the more hostile end of the island, inviting Punic naval intervention.

It occurred between Cape Ecnomus (Monte Rufino) and westerly Heraclea. Hannibal, whose negligence in northern waters had so encouraged the Romans, had been arrested and executed by his officers. Now under two commanders, Hamilcar and Hanno of Acragas, the Carthaginian fleet was arrayed in a single line at right-angles to the coast: an immense pier of more than 300 vessels stretching from inshore to far at sea.

The Romans approached in wedge formation, their leaders, the consuls Atilius Regulus and Manilius Vulso, aiming to bulldoze their way through the attentuated obstacle. Of the four war squadrons in their armada, two formed the leading edges of the wedge; another completed the triangle in line at rear, towing transports; the last followed in reserve.

Hamilcar appears to have envisaged the envelopment, division and selective destruction of the Romans by tactics exploiting the slow movement of the transports. As the leading squadrons of the wedge accelerated to punch a gap in the Punic line, the vessels confronting them deliberately drew back, urging the Roman oarsmen to greater speed.

Unable to keep pace, the transport-towing squadron fell behind. In its rear, the reserve squadron held its post.

At the same time, the wings of the Carthaginian line encircled the Roman flanks. Hamilcar's manoeuvres had gone well. He had achieved the separation of the enemy fleet into three parts, uncovered the rear of the wedge, and placed his own squadrons in striking posts. He deserved success. That it eluded him seems attributable, in part, to Roman initiative, but more so to the continuing inability of the Carthaginians to cope at close quarters against the crows.

While Hamilcar now engaged the forward section of the Roman fleet with his central squadrons, the Carthaginian left (inshore) swept toward the struggling tow-ships; the right, under Hanno, pounced from seaward on the enemy reserves. Early sources present a blurred picture of what ensued. Evidently the tow-ships cut loose from the transports and may have resumed their position in the Roman wedge, for the Carthaginians surprisingly failed to take it in the rear.

Meanwhile, the reserve squadron stood up beside the transports.

In the age of gunnery, Hanno's ships would have had little difficulty destroying, or driving aground, this isolated section of the Roman fleet. But at a time when only the most primitive of missiles were used at sea (ramming was the principal offensive technique), the Carthaginians could not complete their advantage without drawing in range of the waiting crows. They were hesitant.

The result was a mockery of elegant tactics. Instead of Hanno vanquishing the hard-pressed Roman rearguard and moving on to support Hamilcar, it was his opponents who finally were reinforced – first by Regulus, then Manilius – , Hamilcar having failed against the weight of their squadrons. Hanno, trapped between his would-be victims and their rescuers, now lost many ships. Altogether, the Romans sunk 30 Carthaginian vessels, and captured 64, against 24 of their own destroyed. Rome had a second naval triumph to celebrate.

With a clear passage to Africa, the expedition landed near Aspis (Clupea) on the Cap Bon peninsula, from which region it set about plundering the countryside. Fifty years earlier, Agathocles had found it fertile, rich and defenceless. Things had not changed. Among their booty, the invaders reputedly amassed 20,000 slaves.

Had there been less temptation to pillage, the Romans might have acted more directly against Carthage. As it happened, the summer slipped away and Rome ordered the recall of Manilius with the spoils and much of the armada before winter closed sea communications. Regulus was left to maintain a Roman presence in Africa until the new campaign season and another landing. His force numbered 15,000 infantry, a smaller contingent of cavalry, and 40 ships : still a threat to a state whose troops were almost wholly overseas.

At Carthage, the sufets of the day, Hasdrubal-son-of-Hanno and Bostar, organized a defence force while Hamilcar was summoned from Sicily with 5,500 men. Despite the scratch nature of their army, it was decided to oppose the continuing devastations of Regulus, who had advanced to Adys (Hr Oudna), a mere twenty-five miles from Tunis.

Marching to that locality, the Carthaginians encamped on a hill commanding the Roman position. Regulus, perceiving their strength in mounted troops, immediately attacked them on the eminence where cavalry was inhibited. The superiority of the disciplined Roman legions proved overwhelming. The Punic camp was destroyed, its occupants routed. Regulus now seized Tunis, denying Carthage the interior.

The city's position was serious. Risings had occurred among the tribes of the dependencies. Numidians were harrying the territories. Refugees streamed across the isthmus. Yet there was a brighter side. Agathocles had come so far, to fail dismally. The sea gate was open and Carthage retained the asset of her great wealth, a talisman even now stirring distant forces to her side.

These materialized in the form of a band of Spartan mercenaries led by a professional captain named Xanthippus, a veteran of the Greek wars with great flair and experience. Inspiring both senate and soldiery with confidence, Xanthippus quickly took effective charge of the city's motley army, which he drilled with Spartan thoroughness.

Regulus would have been well advised, at this stage, to rest on his achievements until reinforced. Fortune was running for

the Romans. In ten years of war, with victories in Sicily, at sea
and in Africa, they had suffered no major mishap. For this they
could thank the prudence of commanders whose resolution
was matched by an aweness that Rome had the strength to be
patient. Now the record was about to be shattered, the gains
eroded, by a risk as needless as it was rash.

Fired by success at Adys, Regulus aspired to conquer Carthage before the spring brought a successor and fresh troops to
share the credit. He might, indeed, have won terms to Rome's
advantage from the city, for there were peace discussions. But
his ultimatum was so harsh, his manner so arrogant, that the
Carthaginians refused to conclude the talks with a bargain.

His real blunder was in giving battle to the army organized
by Xanthippus, a profoundly different force to that worsted at
Adys. In size, it was much the same as that of Regulus, but its
components offered it tactical advantages. While the Romans
had no more than 500 horse, the Carthaginians had 4,000. They
also possessed 100 elephants, animals the Italians had yet to
meet with confidence.

Regulus dominated in infantry; nevertheless, the 12,000
Carthaginian foot troops were not contemptible. In part, they
comprised the veteran mercenaries of Hamilcar, and the
Spartans. But the greater number were citizens trained by
Xanthippus – inexperienced in war, but high in motivation
and intelligence. It was a rare event: one of the few occasions
when Carthage fielded a largely citizen army.

Regulus doomed his troops from the start by two errors. 1,
He accepted battle on level ground ideal for cavalry (it was
actually chosen, between Carthage and Tunis, by Xanthippus),
a measure of his over-confidence since Adys. 2, He packed his
infantry deep and close before the elephants in the belief that
pachydermous bulk might be offset by concentration.

Both mistakes were disastrous. The elephants, leading the
Carthaginian advance, created havoc in the dense ranks confronting them. The Carthaginian cavalry, brushing aside the
small body of opposing horse, attacked the Romans in flank
and rear.

Those of Regulus's legions who survived the elephants were faced with the unbroken ranks of Punic infantry –'the Carthaginian phalanx,' as Polybius termed it. Encircled and disorganized, the Romans were massacred. About 2,000 legionaries who had driven back the mercenaries on Xanthippus's right escaped to Aspis. Regulus, and a further 500, were captured. The rest perished.

According to legend, Regulus was later released on parole to persuade the Romans to make peace, but, having defiantly advised the senate to pursue war, returned to Carthage and execution. The story, popularized by Horace, appears to be apocryphal. On better evidence, the prisoner died in captivity, his disservice to Rome unredeemed by martyrdom.

The land disaster had a grisly sea sequel. News of Regulus's defeat brought the Roman navy to the aid of the survivors. Repulsing a smaller Punic fleet off Cap Bon, it lifted the remnants of the expedition from Aspis and headed for Sicily. It was July, a month when southerly gales were expected, and the pilots warned against a lee shore. Unwisely, their superiors insisted on lingering to harry the south coast of the island.

They had reached Camarina, between Ecnomus and Cape Pachynus, when a violent storm drove the fleet on the rocks, destroying more than 250 vessels. Possibly, as many as 100,000 crewmen and troops were drowned. Certainly, it was the worst catastrophe at sea known to contemporaries. 'History,' wrote Polybius, 'can scarcely afford another disaster on such a scale.'

16: *Farewell Sicily*

THE First Punic War dragged on another fourteen years, now a conflict of punishing attrition centred once more on Sicily. The Pyrrhic invasion had steeped Italy in grief for her fallen sons; the Punic War produced mourning on an even more tragic scale. Roman bitterness was not diminished by the knowledge that Carthage, for all her financial investment, risked the lives of relatively few of her own menfolk.

Each fresh casualty-list deepened resentment of the Punic state. Sicily swallowed manpower like some massive pit, and Punic money followed. The sacrifice would stop when Rome's vigour was exhausted, Carthage's treasure spent. Until then, it continued with fluctuating fortunes on both sides, the flair of Punic generalship insufficient to surmount the reserves of its dogged foe.

On land, the struggle was of two distinct types: siege warfare, the Romans seeking to reduce Carthage's strongholds in western Sicily; and what might best be described as a *guerilla* war in which the Carthaginians held the initiative, mounting surprise attacks and raids from hill bases. Major field battles were conspicuously absent.

At first, this omission reflected the fear of elephants transmitted to the Roman troops from Africa. Following the defeat of Regulus, the commander of the Carthaginian forces in Sicily, Hasdrubal-son-of-Hanno, had 140 elephants at Lilybaeum. For two years they assured him command of the countryside. Roman morale was low. Then, in 251, Hasdrubal rashly employed the animals against a walled town, Panormus, which had fallen to Rome some years earlier.

Emboldened by their fortifications, the defenders allowed the elephants to draw close before assailing them with arrows and javelins. The tormented beasts ran amok. Confusion in

Hasdrubal's ranks, resulting in his repulse, was overshadowed by the loss to Carthage of the elephants, most of them escaping to be caught by the Romans.

Confident again of appearing on open land, the legions converged against Lilybaeum. From 250, the attackers spared no effort to reduce the stronghold, a base vital to the Punic cause. It was menaced by siege works and armed camps. Its towers were mined; its walls battered by great rams. The officers of the mercenary garrison were suborned.

Against this onslaught, the Carthaginian commander, Himilco, fought a brilliant and fierce defence. With counter-mines and forays, he drove the besiegers back while the bastions were rebuilt to block fresh attacks. He used fire against the enemy. Winning the loyalty of the rank-and-file mercenaries, he thwarted conspiracy, expelling the traitors from the city.

At the end of the summer, a violent gale wrecked some of the wooden towers brought forward by the Romans. Himilco made good use of the chaos. His fire parties sallied against the siege-works in three places, setting light to the tinder-dry timber. Strong winds, fanning the flames, gusted smoke in the faces of the besiegers, increasing their distraction. As they struggled to douse the fires, Himilco's archers bombarded them with arrows.

In the end, the siege-works were completely destroyed: even the metal heads of the battering rams had melted. The Romans now lost faith in assault, relying on blockade. But hopes of starving the city dwindled as supplies continued to arrive by sea.

Meanwhile, the Carthaginians moved their headquarters to Drepana, a port twenty-five miles north of Lilybaeum. Expressive of Roman frustration at this period (though of questionable veracity) is the familiar story of the martinet Roman commander P. Claudius Pulcher who, when the sacred chickens refused to eat – a bad omen – hurled them impatiently into the sea off Drepana with the injunction, 'Damn well drink, then!' or words to that effect.

It was Claudius's successor, Junius Pullus, who conceived

the notion of occupying Mount Eryx (Mount San Guiliano) close to Drepana, thus commanding the land approach to the port. From this eminence, a height of more than 2,000 feet, the Romans directed operations in the northwest, possessing a temple on the summit and the town of Eryx on the lower slopes.

The land conflict now entered a new phase. In 247, the appointment of an outstanding Carthaginian general to the Sicilian command heralded a change in the style of war. Hamilcar Barca, still a young man, was backed by a formidable family. At a time when many in Carthage pressed the need to develop continental power in North Africa, the Barcids consistently stressed Mediterranean priorities.

The 'African' party, led by a second Hanno the Great, was actually active in the extension of Carthaginian territory as far as Theveste (Tebessa, in modern Algeria) while the Romans besieged Drepana and Lilybaeum. It may be that this was a prudent, if belated, policy, but it diverted resources from Sicily and promoted friction between Hanno and Hamilcar.

Hamilcar, anxious to further Barcid policy, took daring steps. Instead of reinforcing the beleaguered bases of the far west, he installed his troops near Roman Panormus, at a place named Herctae (Monte Pellegrino), a high plateau with cultivable land on top. Herctae was an ideal eyrie from which to harry the Romans. Precipitous of approach, its few paths could easily be defended. The height was cool and healthy. It also possessed access to a natural harbour.

While his ships plundered and ravaged the Italian coast, Hamilcar waged a three-year campaign of land raids, skirmishes and ambuscades which, at one stage, engaged a reputed 40,000 Roman troops. It was a strategy quite new to the Punic War. Without hazarding a single major battle, Hamilcar tied up enough enemy legions to relieve the pressure on Lilybaeum.

Eventually, becoming restricted at Herctae, he embarked on another venture. Coasting his forces west to the region of Mount Eryx, Hamilcar smuggled them past the guard-posts at its base, stormed the Roman-held town, and trapped the

Romans in the temple on the summit. Here, for another two years and more, he operated to the exasperation of the enemy, neutralizing Rome's bid for Drepana.

At last it was clear to the Romans that they could not out-fight Hamilcar. For all the men they had committed, with all the losses they had sustained, victory seemed no closer than it had done six years before. The Carthaginian was too asute to accept a set-piece trial of strength. As long as there were ships to supply his hill base and the Punic ports, Rome's legions could make no headway.

Either the war had to be abandoned or won at sea.

*　　*　　*

Rome's first ambitious naval venture after the Camarina disaster was a raid on the coast of North Africa. It proved a fiasco. The newly-built ships ran aground and had to discard equipment to refloat. Worse, bad weather on the return voyage to Italy brought tragedy. Half the fleet went down in the Tyrrhenian; a fresh blow to Roman hopes of sea mastery.

For some time, they restricted their naval effort to the attempt to seal Lilybaeum. Still success eluded them. Amid the shoals and islands which surrounded the harbour, the blockading fleet was outwitted by better-handled and faster Carthaginian ships. Standing off until the wind was favourable, the blockade-runners would sweep under full sail through the dangerous channels straight into harbour, leaving the Romans fumbling in shoal waters.

Once, a complete convoy of 50 ships gained Lilybaeum in this manner.

Among the most celebrated of the blockade-runners was a brilliant seaman known as Hannibal the Rhodian. Every attempt to intercept him failed until a particularly fast Carthaginian vessel fell into Roman hands, enabling the blockaders to overhaul their quarry and capture him.

Not only did the Carthaginians outsail their opponents, they engaged them with new success. By now, counter-tactics had evolved against Rome's unorthodox naval techniques. The poor performance of Roman ships and crews in tricky waters, especially conspicuous since Camarina, invited exploitation. Claudius presented a perfect opportunity.

In 249, the consul resolved to destroy the Punic fleet at Drepana. The method was to be a surprise attack. Sailing directly into the harbour, Claudius would catch the enemy beached or at anchor. Chickens or no chickens, he might well have succeeded had not the Carthaginian admiral, Adherbal, reacted faultlessly.

Claudius sailed by night, was off Drepana at first light, and, as planned, had entered the channel to the harbour before Adherbal could collect his fleet. But the Carthaginian kept a cool head. Waiting as long as he dared for his crews to muster, Adherbal led them to the open sea by a second channel. Claudius had now to extricate his own ships before they in turn were trapped.

Neither his clumsy vessels nor their seamen were up to the manoeuvre. Some collided. Others lost their oars in the narrow channel. Emerging from the harbour in confusion, the Romans found Adherbal's fleet ranged to seaward, penning them inshore. They had little chance. With every advantage of skill and disposition, the Carthaginians drove their enemies into the shallows where, one after another, they ran aground.

'Seeing what was happening, Claudius slipped away, escaping along the coast with about 30 ships,' affirmed the ancient source. The rest of his fleet floundered. Ninety-three ships were captured.

While Claudius faced trial in Rome for negligence, his successor, Junius, sailed from Syracuse with a large convoy of supplies for his western troops. Near fateful Camarina, the convoy was intercepted by one of Adherbal's lieutenants, Carthalo. The promised action was forestalled by an approaching storm.

Carthalo, noting the weather-signs, immediately ran for Cape Pachynus, which he doubled to escape catastrophe. The Romans, too slow or complacent to follow, were caught on the

lee-shore where they suffered the fate of their ill-starred compatriots of 255. 'Scarcely a plank remained intact,' Polybius
wrote of the wrecked fleet. It was too much for the Roman
authorities. Fleet after fleet had met destruction at enormous
cost. From now on, treasury expenditure on naval construction
was ruled out.

Ironically, the best Roman fleet of the war was launched in
the face of such obstruction, built in the winter of 243-242
by the subscription of private enthusiasts. Comprising 200
quinqueremes modelled on the ship seized from Hannibal the
Rhodian, it transferred to Sicily under the consul Lutatius
Catulus, a forceful leader who took pains to recruit and train
good crews. The arrival of Catulus off western Sicily sur-
prised the Carthaginians, again accustomed to freedom of the
sea-lanes.

Indeed, when the Carthaginian navy sailed for the island at
the start of the 241 campaign season it was crammed with
provisions for Hamilcar's army. Learning of the enemy fleet,
the Punic admiral, Hanno, planned to outsail it, disembark the
supplies at Eryx, then, with marines provided by Hamilcar,
resume fighting trim. He underestimated the performance of
the new Roman warships. Despite heavy seas, they challenged
him off the Aegates islands.

It was scarcely a battle. Heavily laden, bereft of fighting
crews, the Carthaginian ships were virtually defenceless. Fifty
were sunk and 70 captured by the time the others turned tail.
Returning to Carthage with the survivors, Hanno was crucified: a characteristic but more than usually futile act of ex-
piation since the war was practically over.

The once brimming coffers of Carthage were empty. Without money, there could be no replacements for the Punic fleet;
without a fleet, no provisions for Sicily. The action off the
Aegates obliged Carthage to acknowledge her position. For
some time Hamilcar's mercenaries had gone unpaid, held
together by exceptional generalship. It could not continue.
The struggle for Sicily was finished.

Abandonment of the island was a heavy blow to Carthage,

E

but Rome's own exhaustion made it bearable. When Hamilcar insisted on removing his army with full war honours, the Romans grudgingly acceded. Both sides needed peace, not further argument.

With dramatic abruptness, the curtain fell. The conflict had lasted twenty-four years, robbed Carthage of the corner-stone of her northern strategy, emptied her treasury. The armistice terms included an indemnity of 3,200 talents payable to Rome over twenty years. Rome, too, had been drained of funds, but her greater loss was in human life. In two decades her citizen population had decreased by something like seventeen per cent; an injury doubtless shared by many allied states.

Militarily, Carthage had performed well. Thanks to the continuity of command in her forces – as opposed to the annual changes of leadership under the Roman consular system – her commanders had repeatedly out-generalled their opponents. Nor were her heterogeneous armies overwhelmed by their more unified and disciplined enemies.

What defeated Carthage in the long run was not any lack of martial ability but the immense numerical predominance of Roman and Italian troop reserves: resources unmatched in the world of the Mediterranean. A generation later, according to Polybius, more than 750,000 men were liable to bear arms for Rome. It is revealing of the recuperative capacity of Carthage that she was yet to cast terror into such a power.

20: *Hamilcar Barca*

WITH the conclusion of fighting in Sicily, Hamilcar relinquished his command leaving Hanno at Carthage to arrange the disbandment of the mercenaries. As these tough veterans – Libyans, Iberians, Ligurians, Balearians and various western Greeks – arrived in Africa to receive their pay-arrears and discharge, the Carthaginian authorities faltered.

Hamilcar had buoyed his men amid the perils of Sicily with promises of remuneration which, to a balked and impoverished government, seemed impossibly extravagant. In the hope that the troops might accept less, or grow weary of waiting and leave for home, the treasury made a small payment on account and camped the soldiers in the depths of the hinterland.

The ploy, already misconceived to the extent that it placed the discontented Libyan mercenaries in contiguity with their volatile blood-brothers of the interior, was further bungled by Hanno, who personally advised the men to take what they were offered. He was greeted angrily. Not only had he never fought in Sicily, he was the architect of expansion at the expense of the Libyan tribes.

Increasing instead of reducing their demands, the mercenaries now marched ominously toward Carthage. At this, the government panicked. The claims were promptly agreed, and some new ones conceded. But the ethnic grievances of the African troops persisted, the more vociferous for the collapse of the authorities over pay.

Among the militants, a Libyan soldier named Matho assumed leadership, predicting the victimization of the Africans if the overseas mercenaries dispersed. His call for unity was backed by an opportunistic Italiot, Spendius. At a series of violent meetings of their followers, troops who wavered were coerced or murdered.

When the Carthaginian paymaster, Gisco, and his assistants were made captive, sedition became open mutiny : a development quickly followed by Libyan insurrection as Matho's envoys stirred up the local tribes. Volunteers arrived in their thousands with provisions and silver to sustain the fight. It was now a major rising. The rebels even struck their own coins, some inscribed with the word 'Libyon.'

Dividing their forces, the insurgents besieged Utica and Hippo Acra, and cut the roads to Carthage. Hanno, taking the field in 240 with citizen troops and newly-raised mercenaries, did nothing to abate the crisis to which he had contributed. The Carthaginians then recalled Hamilcar to service, creating a second army, smaller than Hanno's, for his command.

Hamilcar swiftly showed his brilliance. Twice he beat substantially larger armies under the renegade Spendius, partly by enlisting the support of a Numidian chief named Navaras, to whom he betrothed his daughter as a premium. But he needed a larger force for definitive victory, and Hanno controlled most of the loyal troops. Implacably hostile, the Punic generals disagreed on joint action and merely quarrelled at their meetings.

At last the senate, convinced of the need for a supremo, left the choice to the army. It voted for Hamilcar.

The decision was fatal for the rebels, who resorted increasingly to barbaric practices. Hamilcar, respected if feared by his former troops, had begun by appealing to old loyalties. He showed no vindictiveness, inviting his prisoners to join his army or, alternatively, offering them safe conduct to leave the land. The rebel leaders stood in danger of losing a psychological struggle.

Conscious of Hamilcar's magnetism, they took desperate steps to prevent the mass defection of their followers. Seven hundred Carthaginian prisoners, including Gisco and his officers, were atrociously mutilated by order of the leaders and thrown alive into an open grave. Those among the rebels who protested were also butchered. Henceforward, it was insisted, all captives should be tortured and murdered.

The measure achieved its purpose. Implicated in a crime beyond pardon, the wavering mutineers had no choice but to fight on. The Carthaginians in their fury showed no mercy, trampling their own prisoners now beneath elephants. Hamilcar's 'hearts and minds' campaign was forgotten. He pursued his erstwhile soldiers with grim intent.

First he stalked Spendius, trapping his force in the interior where it was reduced to such pitiful hunger that its members resorted to cannibalism. Tricking Spendius himself into captivity, Hamilcar wiped out the starving and leaderless rebels. He now turned to Matho, who was near Tunis with the rest of the mercenaries. The savagery continued. Spendius was crucified; Matho responded with atrocities.

The last hundred years of Carthaginian history was opening on a note of horror surpassed only by the terror of the final days. Polybius condemned the so-called War of the Mercenaries as unique in his knowledge of human cruelty. The outcome was in little doubt. After a last retreat toward the east coast, Matho was lured into a defile, ambushed, his force annihilated. It was 239 – within a generation of Zama.

Though the rebellion confirmed the Romans in their view of Punic cruelty, Carthaginian excesses were much provoked, and confined to the hour itself. The punishment of African towns which had joined the rebels seems not to have been severe.

*   *   *

While the Mercenary War raged, another group of troops mutinied: the garrison of Carthaginian Sardinia. In 238, frightened by the fate of the rebels in Africa, the Sardinian force invited the Romans to the island. The chance to secure the Tyrrhenian and her own shores was more than Rome could resist. Despite opposition from the native Sardinians, the island was occupied. Rome then legalized her position by forcing Carthage to relinquish her Sardinian rights under threat of renewed war.

This blatant display of power politics, condemned even by Roman apologists, stirred Carthaginians to passionate resentment. Patriotic sentiments based on the tradition of mercantile empire flourished, and with them the Barcids, whose policies recalled better days. Hanno had lost ground through the Truceless War. His party, disinclined to tread on Roman toes, continued to lose support, while Hamilcar, outstanding among the Barcids, rose to fresh heights.

Appointed sole general of Carthage in 237, he promptly demonstrated his commitment to bold enterprise.

Economic and military debility ruled out an immediate Punic challenge to Rome, but there was still a region of the Mediterranean, believed Hamilcar, in which Carthage might recoup wealth and strength without unduly alarming the Romans. Spain, the original magnet of the westering Phoenicians, remained largely uncolonized. Here, in mines, manpower and timber, were virtually limitless resources.

There were other attractions. The shores of Spain were far enough from both Rome and Carthage to allow development without interference. In Spanish bases, Barcid leadership might prevail irrespective of the vagaries of metropolitan politics. Iberian projects would be explained to the Romans as a means of raising wealth to pay the war indemnity.

Hamilcar's vision roamed. Though remote, Spain presented great strategic potential. On her eastern coast were fine natural harbours from which, in conjunction with Balearic and African bases, an important part of the western Mediterranean might still be controlled for Carthage. Even without naval power, it would be possible for Punic arms to operate offensively against Rome from the peninsula by way of Gaul.

In short, the loss of Sicily could be made good by the acquisition of an asset which gave Carthage precisely those military advantages which had served the Romans so well : a vast and accessible reserve of fighting men, and an overland route to their objectives.

There were two problems. With the Punic navy in tatters, Hamilcar had to get his army to Spain without the use of a fleet. Once there, he would have to contend with hostile tribes prepared to defend their lands tenaciously. The first obstacle was overcome by marching west along the north shore of Africa and crossing the straits at Gibraltar with the few ships available as ferries. Hamilcar reached Gades, the old Phoenician depot, in 236, consolidating Carthaginian interests there.

The problem of tribal opposition was less tractable. For some eight years, Hamilcar fought his way tirelessly east then north as far as Alicante, which he founded as Acra Leuce (Lucentum). Intimidated by his brilliance, and won by cajolery, an increasing number of native chiefs, the *caudillos*, joined him as the campaigns proceeded. Fittingly, Hamilcar died an heroic death, saving his companions from drowning in a swollen stream.

The presiding genius in Spain for the next few years was his lieutenant, Hasdrubal Pulcher. Diplomatically talented, Hasdrubal married a Spanish girl, cemented the loyalty of many tribes, and raised New Carthage (Cartagena) as the capital of the dominion at the best harbour on the east coast. From here, with customary industry, the Carthaginians exploited the resources of the territory.

At Cartagena itself, at Huelva on the Gulf of Cadiz, and elsewhere, they worked mines which are still in existence. They cultivated saltings and established a fish-curing industry. They produced and exported esparto grass. Militarily, they recruited and trained Spaniards as mercenaries, and formed alliances with Spanish chiefs.

So far, Rome had accepted the proposition that Carthage needed the new commercial field to pay her war debt. The Romans had no Spanish or Gallic territories, and such concern as they felt at the development probably centred on Massalia, across the Pyrenees from Iberia, the Greek colony through which they imported tin. Without northern tin to add to their copper, it was impossible to make bronze, the rustproof alloy essential to armaments.

By 226, positive misgivings had been stirred by Hasdrubal's expansion toward northern Gaul. Gaul was hostile to Rome.

If, in alliance with Carthage, she marched east, Massalia and Rome's tin supplies would be endangered. An understanding was demanded with Hasdrubal. Accordingly, a treaty was negotiated by which the Carthaginians agreed to confine their forces south of the river Ebro. The *quid pro quo* is unknown, but most likely the Romans, too, accepted the river as the limit of their martial sphere. Certainly, recognition of Punic privilege to its south was implicit.

Such was the position in the year 221, when Hasdrubal's death brought a Barca to power again in Punic Spain. Hannibal, the eldest of Hamilcar's four sons, had been too young to take command on his father's death. Now twenty-five, he was the choice of the army in the peninsula and the popular assembly at Carthage. According to Livy, Hannibal had been made to swear undying enmity to Rome by his father. Be that as it may (and it does not seem improbable), no man was to kindle more hatred in the Romans; none more nearly eradicate the Roman state.

21: *Beyond the Alps*

LONG after the destruction of Carthage the memory of Hannibal haunted the Romans. To Horace he was 'the perfidious,' the 'dread Hannibal,' likened to a wrecking storm or a forest fire. Neither calumny nor the belittlement of his skills exorcized the ghost. Little wonder that the generation of Cato, which fought him, or the children who absorbed its tales, were apprehensive of the city which produced his kind.

The Second Punic War – the War of Hannibal as the Romans called it – remains one episode in Carthaginian history known to everyone, needing slight evocation in these pages. The famous march through the Alps has passed into legend along with many tales of the ordeals encountered there.

Responsibility for the war is arguable. For some time the Romans had encouraged a friendly administration in the Iberian port of Saguntum, perceiving its potential as a bridgehead in eastern Spain. Claiming that the place was under their protection, they threatened war should Hannibal lay siege to it. Two years after succeeding Hasdrubal, he did just that. Saguntum, well to the south of the Ebro, was now the only town in the province which resisted him. It was not in the sphere denied Punic troops by the Roman treaty (i.e., north of the Ebro), nor is there evidence that Rome reserved special rights at Saguntum by any agreement.

But if Rome's ultimatum had no basis in legality, Hannibal's contempt for it scarcely showed aversion for the war he risked. A renewal of the struggle with Rome was implicit not only in his heritage but in his conviction that, from Spain, he could succeed where Carthage had failed before. He would do so by striking at the heart of Rome's power, her dominion in Italy, looking to the Italians to cast off her yoke and take side with him.

E*

By crossing the Ebro in early summer 218, Hannibal anticipated the declaration of war already resolved in Rome. Securing the northeast passage of Spain in a few weeks, he passed
the Pyrenees near the coast into southern France, reaching the
Rhône late in August. Many Gallic recruits joined his army,
the rest of which was mainly of Spaniards and Africans.

Among its best units were the bands of Numidian horsemen
whose aggression and endurance were unexcelled. There was
also Spanish cavalry. Distinct from the Numidians, who liked
to lead remounts into battle and change ponies when one
tired, the Iberians commonly rode two men to a horse, one
rider dismounting to fight on foot. Of interest in the foot ranks
were Balearian slingers, renowned for their aim with lead or
stone missiles. Armed with two types of sling – for long range
and short range – their fire could be more withering than that
of ancient bowmen.

Rome cast her first challenge to Hannibal on the Rhône.
Disembarking at Massilia, the Scipio brothers Publius Cornelius
(father of 'Africanus') and Gnaeus deployed their forces on the
right bank only to find that Hannibal had already crossed the
river and eluded them. Rather than ship the army beyond the
Alps to meet the enemy, the Scipios now took a gamble.

While Publius sailed alone for Pisa to alert northern Italy,
Gnaeus proceeded with the fleet and army to eastern Spain,
where Hannibal's young brother Hasdrubal Barca now held
command. The Roman invasion of Spain at this moment, if
remote from the main drama, would be seen in due course as
a telling move.

Hannibal descended from the Alps to the Po lands, seemingly
by the Dora Riparia, with 20,000 infantry and 6,000 cavalry.
The mountain crossing, though an impressive achievement,
was not unique, for the warlike tribes of Gaul had done it
many times. Nor did elephants, inseparable from Hannibal
in popular imagination, play a major role. Only 37 began the
trek, far fewer than those deployed by Carthage in earlier
campaigns.

Legend has overdone the hardships. That more than 50,000

men – the traditional estimate – were lost between the Ebro
and the Po is inconceivable in the light of Hannibal's competence. The speed and success with which he took the offensive in northern Italy points to a force in good shape and heart,
not the remnants of a marathon massacre. Almost at once,
the invaders overwhelmed the stronghold of the hostile Taurini
Gauls, then, gathering friendly tribes, moved down the Po
toward the newly-formed Roman colonies of Placentia
(Piacenza) and Cremona.

Scipio, having taken command of two legions in the area,
had advanced to a northern tributary, the Ticino. Here, a
cavalry skirmish, demonstrating the superiority of the Numidians over the Roman horse, led to the injury of Scipio, who
withdrew south of the Po to the Trebia. He was now reinforced
by some 20,000 troops under his fellow consul Tiberius
Sempronius, hot-foot from Sicily and an impending blow at
Africa.

It was December. The water was icy as Sempronius threw
his legions across the Trebia and into the first major battle
for Italy. At the end of the day, no more than 10,000 legionaries scrambled back through the stream to Placentia. The
greater part of the Roman force was dead or captured.
Sempronius, pleading storm and flood to excuse himself, ignored the fact that he had been out-manoeuvred at every stage
on ground picked by Hannibal precisely for its natural snares.

Trebia closed a momentous year with the Carthaginian
commanding most of the territory north of the Appenines,
through which he could choose his passage the next spring.
The campaign had won to his side not only a host of anti-
Roman Celts but a number who had formerly served Rome.
Above all, it had fulfilled the strategic purpose of averting an
offensive against Carthage by concentrating Roman forces in
the north. The new year would find Rome on the defensive in
Italy.

Two armies were posted to check a Punic advance south,
one on the east coast at Ariminum (Rimini), the other across
the Appenines at Arretium (Arezzo). Hannibal, having win-

tered at Bologna, avoided both by what Polybius termed 'a difficult short cut'– probably the Collina pass and the marshes of the Arno, then in spring flood – to appear in Etruria.

While the Carthaginian marched boldly through the north-east, the Roman commander at Arretium, Gaius Flaminius, stood by inactively. Polybius characterises Flaminius as a military nincompoop, but he was perhaps not unwise in delaying an attack on Hannibal until his colleague at Ariminum, Gnaeus Servilius, might join him. Servilius was in fact approaching by forced marches when Hannibal, having swung round Arretium, headed back into the hills as if making to challenge the advancing force.

At last Flaminius felt safe in following. He had reached the north shore of Lake Trasimene, and was marching in morning mist through the narrow Borghetto pass, when he beheld the trap set for him. Hannibal had placed his troops in ambush during the night. At a signal, they attacked from all sides, blocking the pass and swarming down the valley slopes. The Romans, caught in line of march, had no chance. Flaminius was killed, his army massacred.

Servilius, unable to get his main force near enough to help, had sent 4,000 mounted troops ahead. Somewhere near Assisi, the contingent was intercepted by Hannibal's cavalry leader, Maharbal, and wiped out.

News of the defeats produced consternation at Rome. The elderly senator Fabius Maximus was appointed dictator in the crisis, religious invocations were intensified, defences strengthened. But Hannibal avoided Rome. His army was sore and weary. Veering east to the Adriatic plains, the invaders rested during mid-summer, bathing their wounds, then resumed campaigning to the south, ravaging Apulia and Campania.

Fabius took the prudent view that Hannibal and his army were too good to be confronted in full array. Instead, the dictator adopted a policy of attrition, dogging the enemy's movements, harassing detachments and supply details. On no account was battle to be offered on equal terms, or on the terms of Hannibal. Roman impatience, aroused by Fabian strategy, was not mollified by the audacity with which the enemy outwitted his shadowers.

In the most famous instance of Hannibalic ingenuity, the Callicula pass engagement, the general extricated his force from ambush by stampeding cattle toward the Romans after dark. By 216, frustration at Rome, expressed in demands for decisive action, was preparing the ground for Hannibal's third, and last, great victory.

Early in June, seeking provisions, the invaders seized a Roman supply base at Cannae, near the Ofanto river. Here, they were approached by the consuls of the year, Lucius Aemilius Paulus and Gaius Terentius Varra, with a Roman army of impressive strength. Even allowing for exaggeration in the traditional estimate of 80,000 men, it probably exceeded Hannibal's 50,000, and certainly preponderated in infantry. In cavalry, the Carthaginians were stronger.

Authorized to give battle by a senate tired of Fabian caution, the Romans took position beside the Ofanto in customary or-der: cavalry and allied contingents on the wings, heavy legions in the centre. Hannibal confronted the enemy with his centre advanced and the line drawn back on either side, a crescent with horns pointing to the rear. To the front were Gauls and Spaniards; on their flanks, Africans. His cavalry en-gaged the Roman wings.

The exotic variety of the Punic force impressed the ancient scribes. The Gauls, naked from the waist up, wielded great slashing swords; the Spaniards, shorter chopping and stabbing blades. The latter wore tunics of white with scarlet trimmings. Elsewhere, the Libyans appear to have decked themselves with arms captured in previous victories for, according to Livy, 'one might have taken them for a Roman battle line.'

Military interest in Cannae, however, rests not so much in any particular group or armament but in the classic manoeuvre for which it has become famed.

Hannibal's tactics were based on the expectation that the dense legions at the centre of the Roman formation would drive the Gauls and Spaniards back through the Libyan lines, which would then turn inwards on the legions from either flank. The crescent would no longer be convex but concave, a pincer with the Roman legions in its jaws. Success depended on Hannibal's horsemen taking out the Roman wings – a safe bet, for cavalry was his strong arm – and, crucially, on the Gauls and Spaniards giving ground without breaking.

The manoeuvre worked perfectly. As a final stroke, the Spanish cavalry, leaving the Numidians to complete the rout of the Roman wings, engaged the rear of the legions to complete their encirclement. Aemilius Paulus and eighty senators fell with 25,000 or more legionaries in the deadly ring. Another 10,000 of their side were killed or captured later. Hannibal's losses, about one to six of the enemy's were mostly in men of the Gallic tribes.

Cannae represented Rome's darkest hour in the Punic wars. Until now, the Italic confederation had remained intact. Neither Trebia nor Lake Trasimene, though alarming, had actually detached components from the Roman alliance. It took Cannae to crack the structure, topple its weakest towers. First Arpi (Foggia), in northern Apulia, defected, then a string of Samnite, Lucanian and Bruttian communities. Lastly, the great Campanian centre of Capua, second city of the peninsula, broke away, promised autonomy – ultimately, the hegemony of Italy – by Hannibal.

At Capua the Punic army went into winter quarters and, as legend had it, surrendered its fighting spirit to the pleasures of the neighbourhood. It is true that Hannibal's spectacular successes were not resumed; that Cannae may be seen as a watershed. But the general's failure to exploit his triumph was due to factors altogether more weighty than the seductions of Campania.

With a single army of limited proportions, lacking siege machines, dependent on the land for supplies, Hannibal could not hope to reduce the defences of Rome itself. The one measure that could conclude the war at a stroke was beyond his means. Instead, he was obliged to attempt further inroads on the confederacy, at the same time protecting the defected cities of Campania and Apulia – a responsibility that diminished his offensive flexibility, substituting defensive needs foreign to his genius.

For their part, the Romans responded to Cannae with grim resilience. After an initial outbreak of panic and some human sacrifice (a number of foreigners and a Vestal Virgin were buried alive), the people showed their remarkable tenacity. Boys and even slaves were enlisted to replace shattered armies; taxes doubled to save a sinking treasury. Auspiciously, the government readopted the strategy of Fabius. This time, it brought results. Rome's capacity at least to win back towns in one theatre while the foe was in another, improved morale. Hannibal was at last seen to have his own difficulties.

High among them was the problem of manpower. In his eagerness to win Italian friends, the Carthaginian promised them freedom from army service. Thus his casualties and sick could be replaced locally only by volunteers, and they were few indeed. Help from Carthage was meagre. The Barcids had planned a land war, and Rome never relinquished command at sea. Nevertheless, after Cannae two expeditions were fitted out in Africa for Italy, one limited to cavalry reinforcements and some elephants.

While the latter, under a commander named Bomilcar, slipped through to Hannibal, the larger force was diverted to Spain at the news of Roman gains there. Other Punic troops landed in Sardinia and Sicily. On the former, they got nowhere. In Sicily, the death of Rome's old ally, Hiero of Syracuse, produced widespread rebellions which the Carthaginians exploited hopefully until the rugged Roman general Claudius Marcellus entered Syracuse.

Hannibal had expected to receive all the reinforcements he needed by land from Spain. The inspired intervention of the Scipios – in some ways the Roman counterpart of the Barcid family – put a stop to that. Gnaeus, with the first expedition to eastern Spain, was not a great soldier but capable of establishing a footing against the new commander of the province, Hasdrubal Barca. In 210 the brilliant 'Africanus' arrived to seize Cartagena (209) and defeat Hasdrubal at Baecula (Bailén) in 208.

Hasdrubal spared no effort but was lacking in maturity. Disengaging from Scipio, he made a brave attempt to join his kinsman in Italy but was vanquished and slain after crossing the Alps by a Roman army forewarned of his intentions. His head was delivered to his brother by the Romans.

All considered, it is a tribute to extraordinary ability that, for a decade after Cannae, Hannibal maintained his undefeated record in Italy, eluding larger forces, snatching local successes, always waiting for the backing that never came. Livy wrote of his achievement:

> For thirteen years he waged war far from home, not with an army of his own countrymen but with a miscellaneous crowd gathered from many nations – men who had neither laws, nor customs, nor language in common, differing in costume, arms, worship and even gods. And yet he kept them together by so close a tie that they never fought among themselves or mutinied against him, though he was often without money for their pay. Even after Hasdrubal's death, when he had only a corner of Italy left to him, his camp was as orderly as ever.

Finally, another brother, Mago Barca, forsaking Spain, sailed to Liguria by Minorca (Port Mahon – Mago's Harbour – commemorates the visit) to rally the Gauls to his banner. As a diversion in Hannibal's favour, the bid failed. Scipio did not. Persuading a reluctant senate to allow his invasion of Africa, he landed in 204 and besieged Utica. Carthage, in alliance with Masinissa's rival, Syphax of Numidia, challenged Scipio. He made sport of them. Burning their camps as a preliminary, he routed the Carthaginians at Souk el-Kremis, on the upper Bagradas.

In the autumn of 203, allegedly a bitter man, Hannibal sailed from Italy to the aid of his native land – and to Zama.

22: *Economic Revival*

As already recounted, Rome and Carthage lived at peace for half a century after Zama. Sedulously, the Carthaginians paid their war debts. Industriously, the people wrought an 'economic miracle.' Like the great flocks of doves which sometimes arrived to join the birds in the temple precincts – the ancients thought they accompanied the gods on their travels – prosperity settled again on the Punic realm.

In the country estates of the landed proprietors, bright flowers blossomed among olive and fig trees, emblems of divine blessing, the supply source of questing bees. Carthaginian bees were valued not only for their honey but for the reputedly superior quality of the wax produced, used in medicine and encaustic art. Little was wasted on the limited growing lands of the *chora*, the agricultural region of Carthage.

The proprietor, surveying his irrigated orchards, his longhorned cattle, his domesticated gazelles and ostriches, from the cool logia which perhaps overlooked a lagoon in which flamingoes fed, was no absentee landlord in the style of the Roman *latifundiary*. Like his city brother, the Carthaginian country gentleman was a profit-conscious master dedicated to increasing production. Not the least of the exertions expended in field and orchard were his own.

In the city itself, amid thoroughfares teeming with seamen, traders, factory workers, market-gardeners from the Megara, the same devotion to productivity was evident. Pottery, the chief medium of working utensils, was manufactured and sold on a vast scale – the thousands of jars and pitchers devoted to the dead representing a constant market, let alone those for industrial and domestic use.

Seldom a 'quality' manufacturer, the Carthaginian potter concentrated on mass production of low-priced articles. Punic kilns, connected with workshops, cellars and storerooms, were much like those still used in Tunisia. One pottery discovered in modern times in a well-preserved condition contained thousands of vessels of various shapes and sizes awaiting sale.

The industry also supplied cheap religious imagery, figurines and even life-size statues, in clay, some cast from Greek models. The devotion of the Mediterranean peoples to divine objects, commonly placed in houses, private chapels and graves, or used as offerings at temples, created a continuous demand for terracotta gods and goddesses which Punic workshops met by the gross. They did a brisk trade, too, in pottery medallions depicting deities.

The largest employers of craftsmen in Carthage, especially in wartime, were the armaments and shipbuilding industries. The number of employees for the Carthaginian arsenal is not known, but it has been estimated that there were about 1,600 metal workers, probably in several workshops, and a substantial force of carpenters making siege machines, shafts for javelins, and so on. It seems likely that the total would have been somewhat greater than that for the provincial arsenal at Cartagena, which employed 2,000 people (according to Polybius).

In peacetime, many armourers and carpenters switched from state to private employment. Metal workers made tools, domestic appliances, bronze utensils and ornaments. Again plentiful and cheap, their articles were not of sterling class. Despite Carthage's trade in raw metals, no attempt was made to sell finished products overseas.

Her woodworkers, on the other hand, were known for their quality. Solomon had valued the skill of Phoenician carpenters, and the early African colonists had found timber in the new lands well-suited to building and repairing ships. Unlike their compatriots in the metal industry, shipbuilders could move from military to civil work of the same kind, simply shifting from naval to merchant yards.

When shipbuilding was depressed, there were ploughs to make for farmers (Carthaginian ploughs were wooden, without wheels, as still found in North Africa), threshing-sleds (the ingenious 'Punic cart' as the Romans called it), household chests, and other timber items.

The manufacture of fabrics was assiduously organized. Apart from self-supporting spinning and weaving within Carthaginian families, there were professional spinners and large workshops where dozens of slaves were kept busy. Dyeing, too, was a regular industry. So popular was the purple extract from the shell-fish *murex* that, even today, piles of broken shells mark the sites where the dye vats were sited. Red dye was used on hide to make a type of morocco – a process probably learned from nomads of the interior.

It was not the talent of specific Carthaginians which Cato, on his visit of 152, remarked nervously. Punic society mistrusted outstanding individuals, particularly in the field of politics, where the failure of aspiring tyrants was conspicuous. What disturbed the Roman was the remarkable diligence and civic solidarity which gave Carthage her resilience, her capacity to regenerate wealth and strength in the aftermath of blows that would have crushed the vigour of other states.

Behind the multi-coloured populace swarming docklands, arsenals, factories, offices, was a system – not lacking institutional tyrannies – impelling all classes toward the supreme state objective of acquiring wealth. That private wealth, as in all ancient societies, was cruelly ill-distributed, appears not to have created serious friction in the city. The few recorded incitements to revolt completely failed to arouse the proletariat. Even the slaves, who must have been numerous, showed no inclination to rebel. Indeed, their loyalty was a source of strength in the last crisis.

So far as the system was endangered by social discontent, trouble lay in the native communities of Carthage's African territories: the Libyan farmers who paid high rents and taxes, and would have preferred, in any case, to return to the nomadic life across the frontiers. Such people were always potential allies for invaders, and had made havoc by joining the disgruntled mercenaries after the First Punic War.

Carthage herself avoided the social turmoils of the Greek states. Perhaps the lack of an idle aristocracy contributed to a sense of common purpose. Just as landowners laboured on their own soil, so lords of industry and heads of state remained practical men involved in workaday problems. Industrious and businesslike, the upper-class encouraged its sons to start their careers at a humble level and work up. Such customs made for the respect of subordinates.

Certainly, esteem attached to the leaders of religion, a factor central to social solidarity. The priests of Baal Hammon, Melkart, Eshmoun, and other gods, interceded for the city with terrifying forces. Their job was not enviable. The placating of a deity could as well demand the slaughter of a priest, a *kohen*, as that of any other life. One priest of Melkart was sacrificed by crucifixion in his vestments, despite being the son of a Punic king.

For all *kohanim*, the rigours of everyday life were formidable. Some priests wore the yoke, like common prisoners. Others, completely shaven, went barefoot in coarse robes. Not all were dedicated to celibacy, but all observed endless taboos to ward off dangers. As with others in positions of influence, the priests were carefully watched by the Punic state, in their case by a board of ten magistrates.

Yet if toil and austerity, cupidity and oppressive gods, were ingredients in Carthaginian society, there was a less daunting side to the picture. At annual festivals and frolics, even the priestly orders let their hair down. A sacred banquet depicted on the funeral stone of a priestess shows people lying on couches beside food and wine. The figure of a woman attired in nothing but brassière and ear-rings suggests a far from forbidding scene.

Rare figurines expressing life naturalistically, if crudely – a peasant in woollen *djellaba*, a well-to-do fellow sporting a cape over an embroidered tunic, the ubiquitous and burdened donkey – have survived to evoke familiar and captivating associations for those who know North Africa.

Like all people, the Phoenicians delighted in pretty objects, sometimes of slight utility, especially of personal adornment. A humble bone-worker was buried at Utica wearing an elaborate gold-filigree ear-ring and a necklace with five pendants. Beside him were mother-of-pearl shells, polished stones and carved medallions.

Brightly-coloured glassware, characteristically of dark blue fused with brilliant yellow, was a feature of Carthaginian craftsmanship. It took many forms: beads, small phials, scarabs and a variety of charms for warding off the evil eye. Glass-blowers, jewellers, carvers of ivory and wood, and other practitioners of the decorative crafts, were numerous. There was even a group which painted faces and patterns on ostrich eggs. Cheap and repetitive their goods may often have been; dull, they were not.

It was across this bustling and assiduous society – again prosperous but no longer, in the 2nd century, a power in the class of Rome – that there fell after more than four decades of peace the shadows of Masinissa and Cato: old men, hoary survivors of distant battles, refusing to let the past die. In 149, as the consuls Manilius and Censorinus landed their army at Utica, Cato was eighty-five, Masinissa eighty-nine. Neither would survive the year, but their damage was already done.

Had unusual longevity not been bestowed on them, the destruction of Carthage might never have been proposed.

As it was, Cato had drained his energy translating his objective into action – and then, with the city duped into virtual defencelessness, the consuls could not deliver the death-blow in his lifetime. Carthage was yet to write her last chapter in epic terms. That she survived the shock of Rome's treachery to do so was closely bound to the twin attributes of social cohesion and industry.

23: *Arms and Men*

THE declaration of war by Carthage on receiving pronouncement of her intended destruction was not taken very seriously by the Roman consuls. Having achieved the disarming of the city by trickery, Censorinus and Manilius were prepared for a brief storm of fury. It could reasonably be expected to subside as judgement replaced emotion and the citizens resigned themselves to their plight.

An invading army of 80,000 stood ready to march the few miles to Carthage. Offshore, the Roman fleet was prepared to support the advance. Carthage, denied warships by the treaty of 201, had no navy. The remnants of her land force, shattered by Masinissa, skulked in the interior. She had no weapons with which to arm her populace. To complete her distress, not only Utica but a batch of important satellites, including Hadrumetum, Leptis Minor, Thapsus and Acholla, submitted to the enemy.

That Carthage's impulsive defiance was no more than bravura seemed certain to her persecutors when the citizens requested a thirty-day truce in which to make a last appeal to Rome. The consuls rejected the approach. When the city had stewed a while in its helplessness, they would move unopposed to their ordained task. The psychology was persuasive, but ignored the Punic temperament.

Deluded by concessions and pleas into underestimating Punic fibre, the consuls were complacent. True, the Carthaginians, happier bargaining than fighting, were diplomats by inclination, soldiers only in extremity. Pushed too far, however, the Phoenician breed fought ferociously, with a suicidal passion evidenced by the resistance of the Tyrians to the might of Assyria, and by the Motyans in the time of Dionysius.

Beaten now in the war of diplomacy, Carthage was not bluffing. The new government of resistance had popular backing; indeed, was born of public insistence. Every hour of Roman inactivity was put by the citizens to fevered use.

The most important work, when the people recovered from the anguish of their first despair, was the production of weapons to make good the surrendered arms. For this job, the city's work-force, geared to fast utility output, was well equipped. Apart from the regular factories, temples and public buildings were turned into workshops for armaments. Weapons were forged and assembled at a hectic pace.

Knowledge of Carthaginian weaponry is confused by the use in normal times of mercenaries who carried the arms of their own lands. The citizen element of Punic armies seems to have resembled the Greek hoplite forces in drill and equipment, with round-topped, crested helmets, body armour, shields, swords and lances. The statue of a warlike deity at Carthage was clad in a Greek-style cuirass. Punic stelae depict warriors with greaves, round shields and a characteristic short-sword with a V-shaped hand-guard.

At the same time, Roman inventories of captured Punic weapons mention the *scutum*, or oval shield, and there is evidence of long-swords and conical helmets – these probably belonging to light infantrymen rather than heavily-armoured troops. The Sacred Band was renowned for the splendour of its armour and emblems, but doubtless the hardwear produced in the rearmament of 149 was entirely plain and basic to the needs of the emergency.

Carthaginian cavalry was mainly of lightly armed horsemen in the Numidian style, fighting with small shields and javelins. Effectiveness derived from equestrian dexterity, the fleetness of the diminutive barbary mounts and the power and accuracy with which the riders hurled their missiles. There was also a *corps d'élite* of heavy citizen cavalry, the mounted section of the Sacred Band, more elaborately protected than the light horse and apparently equipped with long cavalry swords.

Though archers appear to have played little part in Punic

warfare – bows and arrows are not listed among the items produced in the crisis – the Carthaginians specialized in the projection of various missiles, notably limestone shots hurled from balistae, catapults and other contraptions. Thousands of such munitions, weighing from twelve to more than thirty pounds, have been found on the site at Carthage, produced at the time of the final threat.

The machines employed to project them worked on several principles, including propulsion by metal springs and centrifugal force. Those specifically mentioned as part of the 149 arms drive – probably the simplest to manufacture – were operated by twisting elastic ropes. Such devices were useful defensive weapons, particularly when mounted in elevated positions: on walls and towers. Another Punic war machine, the chariot, was mainly offensive in purpose, at its best in desert fighting, and little use to a beleaguered force.

The most vital of these items now emerged from the factories in a ceaseless flow. Men and women worked day and night. Metal was stripped from houses and public places to augment reserves. Matrons cut off their long hair, recounted Appian, and twisted it into ropes for catapults.

Each day, the workshops produced 100 shields, 300 swords, 500 javelins, and 'as many catapults as they could.' Stone missiles were hewn by the thousand, some for mechanical projection, others to be thrown by hand from the ramparts. It was a remarkable effort. Even so, it would have taken more than eight months to arm the equivalent of the Roman army, and that sketchily with a grave deficiency of protective gear. Wisely, with walls to defend, the Carthaginians placed the emphasis on missile weapons, strikingly javelins.

Meanwhile, the slaves of the city were freed to fight beside the citizens; a measure wholly justified, for the emancipated bondsmen gave brave and true service to the end.

Hasdrubal, the general defeated by Masinissa and condemned by the old government to appease the Romans, was pardoned hastily and instructed to salvage what he could of the field army. Rallying about 20,000 men, he established himself in the interior, guarding the vital route to the grain lands and discouraging Libyan insurrection.

Another Hasdrubal, prominent in the democratic party, initially held command within the city, but little is known of him and he was soon removed by assassination – possibly due to his relationship, through his mother, with Masinissa, who was his grandfather. More conspicuous in the early stages of the defence was a cavalry commander named Himilco Phameas, operating in the country outside the walls.

Impressively, if belatedly, the consuls advanced in early summer from Utica. A Roman army on the move was at any time an awesome spectacle, and this was a force of unusual strength. Typically, a consular army, comprising two Roman legions, two allied legions, and auxiliaries, would have been about 20,000 strong. With a total force of 80,000, Censorinus and Manilius each commanded twice the number of troops to be expected in less exceptional circumstances.

The Roman legion of the period, about 4,500 men, was divided into ten cohorts, each of three maniples. In modern terms, these compared roughly as tactical units with a division, battalions and companies. Traditionally, the troops of the cohort were represented in its maniples on an age basis, one maniple containing the younger men (*hastati*), another somewhat older men (*principes*), and the third containing middle-aged veterans (*triarii*).

All were helmeted and armoured from the waist up. Of the two younger groups, each man was armed with sword, shield, lance and javelin. The veterans fought with swords and pikes. In addition to these units, a company of light infantry and a small troop of cavalry were attached to the cohort. In each army, a force of 1,000 troops (including 200 cavalry) was detached to form the reserve and provide the consul's bodyguard.

Unlike the heavy infantry of Carthage, which fought in a solid phalanx, shoulder to shoulder, in the manner of Greek hoplites, the Roman legionaries stood a pace or two apart, with more room to swing their weapons, while spaces were left between the maniples. The Romans were not outstanding cavalrymen. The strength of their armies was in the part-time but generally enthusiastic legionaries, and the highly-disciplined centurions, tough professional N.C.O.s who served two to a maniple.

Consular command was less reliable. The system still operating by which generals were changed annually – a precaution against military dictatorship – worked against the accretion of martial experience and made coherent strategy difficult for any length of time. The expedition against Carthage was not exempt from this failing.

But to the legions heading southeast for their boasted destination, the prowess of their generals must have seemed irrelevant. The richest city in the world lay before them, ostensibly helpless. The men had enlisted not for the fighting this time, but the pickings, and events so far had buoyed their confidence.

The legionary marched laden. In addition to his weapons and armour, he carried digging tools, cooking pot, rations of corn and meat, and two palisades to contribute to field fortifications. To the legionaries of Censorinus and Manilius, the load was slight discouragement. It would, they hoped, be increased soon with Punic loot.

Coiling inland of the Sebka er Riana, the great lagoon then open to the sea, the invading column swung east on to the isthmus. The heights of Carthage smudged the skyline, straggling south from Catacomb to the Byrsa. To the left of the Romans sparkled the gulf they had skirted; to the right, the lake of Tunis and its marshes. Ahead, spanning the neck between the waters, stretched the city's celebrated landward ramparts, the triple fortifications studded with massive four-storey towers.

Inconsequential to an army which expected the gates to be surrendered, the populace unarmed, these became a different proposition when report indicated the inlets barred and the walls manned by defiant citizens, many of whom possessed newly-forged weapons. They may have seemed to the consuls a contemptible garrison, but they meant that the operation was not to be bloodless.

Deploying their divisions, the Romans prepared to sweep aside the mob.

24: *Repulse*

Manilius threw his troops against the land wall. Since he can scarcely have expected to carry such bulwarks against serious defence, he must have reckoned on the Carthaginians abandoning their posts as the attack commenced. It was, perhaps, a fair assumption. The purposeful and disciplined approach of 40,000 efficiently-equipped soldiers in battle order was a sight to test the resolution of any force, let alone an extemporary levy.

The fighting formation of the Roman army was led by the youngest men. The maniples of *hastati* advanced in twelve files, ten men deep. Between each maniple in the line was a gap equal in distance to the frontage of a maniple. In the second line, composed of the next in age, the maniples were positioned behind the spaces in the line ahead. The third line, of veteran troops, contained smaller maniples (six files, ten men deep) again covering the gaps of the preceding line.

As the youths of the vanguard surged toward the broad ditch and earthwork fronting the great wall, the Carthaginian bombardment would have started. It is not difficult to imagine the effect of the missiles on the advancing ranks. Stones the size of pumpkins hailed on the Romans. Any one of the shots could flatten a man's head, or smash his ribs through his thorax, but the principle purpose of the barrage was to scatter formations and confuse the foe.

Groups of men braving the unexpected pounding were met with showers of smaller shots and javelins from the ramparts. No force could surmount forty-foot walls without siege-machines while the heights were manned. Neither the professional centurions nor the *triarii*, placed to steady the younger troops, can have failed to observe the futility of the assault when the Carthaginians stood their ground.

Carrying their wounded, the legions of Manilius pulled back to encamp, with some humiliation, on the isthmus.

Censorinus directed his own attack against the water-bounded wall which encircled Carthage on her other fronts. Though in itself less forbidding than the triple landward barrier, this gained defensively from the paucity of ground (in some places there was almost none) on which an enemy could manoeuvre between beach and fortification. Censorinus in fact chose the only region with any tactical elbow-room.

At the southeastern point of the city, near the outlet of the harbours to the bay of Kram, a tongue of land protruded outside the wall toward what is now Goletta (Halk el Wad), at the mouth of the channel to Tunis. This tongue, washed on one side by the sea, on the other by the lake of Tunis, was known to the Romans as the *taenia*, the ribbon. It provided an adequate, though not generous, beach-head from which Censorinus could hammer a relatively weak portion of the wall: a portion, moreover, adjacent to the Byrsa, the city's heart.

Even so, he fared no better in attack than Manilius. Again, a storm of missiles struck the Romans, while the citizen defenders rallied fiercely to the sector. Like his fellow general, Censorinus had to draw off and lick his wounds. Notice had been served by their opponents that Carthage intended to die hard. It was frustrating for the consuls, even abashing, but less than devastating. The remedy clearly lay in assault-machines, invaluable adjuncts of siege war.

The Romans had confiscated many at the time of the city's disarming, but they were cumbersome vehicles and the consuls had elected to march 'light.' They now sought timber with which to make good their needs.

There were woods beyond the lake of Tunis, and Censorinus sent working-parties to fetch supplies. Tempting prey for the roving Himilco Phameas and his horsemen, the Roman gangs succeeded in their quest at a painful cost. At least one was severely mauled. But Censorinus got his timber, and machines were constructed. They included two massive battering devices, one of which, according to Appian, was operated and escorted by 6,000 men.

The next snag was the marshy bank of the lake beside the *taenia*, where the wall was weakest and most vulnerable to attack. Laboriously, the Romans packed the ground with stones and firm soil until it was possible to bring the battering-rams to bear in the area. The great engines quickly pounded a breach in the defences, but the Carthaginians, swarming to the danger-spot, repaired the wall overnight. In a sudden foray, they also disabled the siege-machines.

Censorinus, provoked by such audacity, replied by thrusting assault troops through a gap which remained in the damaged wall. The attackers, quickly in difficulty and obliged to withdraw through the narrow exit, owed their escape to a covering action inspired by a young officer soon to rise to prominence – the Scipio Aemilianus noted during the war with Numidia which he witnessed during his trip to buy elephants.

It was now July and the Romans were uncomfortably aware that they were in Africa. Censorinus, camped by the swampy banks of the lagoon, began to lose troops to heat and pestilence. Transferring his men and ships from the fetid waters of the lake to the sea coast across the *taenia*, he encountered more trouble. Familiar with the currents and prevailing winds, the Carthaginians prepared fire-ships in the safety of the bay of Kram then released them to drift to the consul's anchorage. Appian alleged the near-destruction of the Roman fleet.

Plainly, the straightforward reduction of Carthage as envisaged by the aggressors was going wrong. Each day, more weapons flowed from the Punic forges. Emboldened, the defenders dared to sally intrepidly beyond their walls. Himilco menaced the Roman supplies with his cavalry. A review of strategy had become urgent in the consuls' camp.

One striking omission in Roman plans had been the neglect of Masinissa, a vital ally at Zama and more recently the scourge of Hasdrubal's army. In their confidence, the consuls had dismissed the Numidian. 'When we need you, we'll let you know,' he had been told.

Not that the old King was eager to take sides. For years he had dreamed of Carthage as his own prize; now Rome meant to rob him of that dream. With Carthage gone, the usefulness of Masinissa to Rome would have gone, too. If the Romans could smash the Punic empire, certainly they could have their way with a Numidian state isolated in North Africa. Resentfully, Masinissa brooded at Cirta.

One reason his importance was now recognized by the invaders was their growing concern with Hasdrubal. While Carthage had been thought to fall like a ripe plumb, the Punic troops of the interior had seemed of little consequence. Their collapse would follow that of the metropolis. But the city's resistance had altered their significance.

Based on Nepheris, about eighteen miles south of Carthage, Hasdrubal not only bestrode lines of communication crucial in a long siege, but was a disconcerting force behind the Roman camps. Numerically he lacked the power to intervene directly. His raiding capability, however, was considerable, particularly as expressed by the horsemen led by Himilco. Against these swooping riders the Romans had no answer – except to enlist the aid of Masinissa's cavalry.

The conclusions were twofold. The snubbed Numidian would have to be approached for assistance, and Hasdrubal would have to be neutralized: the second flowing, ideally from the first. An obvious ambassador to the old king existed at the Roman camp in the person of Scipio Aemilianus. Masinissa held the memory of his ally 'Africanus' in great respect. Even an adopted member of the Scipionic family could expect to be honoured at Cirta.

But Manilius was impatient. Left in sole command of the siege for the winter while Censorinus returned to Rome for the annual elections, the remaining consul resolved to march on Nepheris without waiting for Numidian assistance. It was perilous. Hasdrubal was a rugged and experienced commander, none the less formidable for having learned a painful lesson from Masinissa. He knew the territory intimately; his troops were campaign veterans; his cavalry was menacing.

While compelled by Roman numbers to avoid a set-piece battle, Hasdrubal might severely embarrass his foes in wild country. And so it happened.

At this stage, the reputation of Scipio Aemilianus takes heroic flight. Remembering that in Polybius he had the outstanding historian of the day as a close friend, it is wise to recognize an element of propaganda in the exploits recounted of the young tribune. At face value, he appears to have upheld the Roman campaign almost single-handed for several months.

Thus, Scipio is credited with disapproving of his superior's plan; with rescuing Manilius and his army from disaster on the futile Nepheris enterprise; with saving four cohorts from massacre on the withdrawal; with persuading Hasdrubal to give decent burial to the Roman dead. Polybius quotes Homer to describe his hero: 'he alone is flesh and blood, the rest are fleeting shadows.'

Improbably, the words are put into the mouth of Cato, an inveterate opponent of Hellenist and Scipionic modes of life. Yet, if some scepticism is valid, Scipio clearly justified a growing reputation.

Leaving soon for Numidia, he arrived at Cirta to find Masinissa dead and the old king's very different sons faced with resolving the succession. It was said that he solved the problem with consummate finesse. At Scipio's suggestion, Micipsa, the oldest of three legitimate sons to have survived, 'a lover of peace,' took charge of the palace and Cirta. The youngest, Mastanubal, a student of law, was assigned the post of justice. The middle son, Gulussa, a warlike prince, was given charge of foreign policy.

With Gulussa's goodwill, Scipio indeed gained a political trump in what was emerging as a bid for control of the whole campaign. Confronting Himilco Phameas with the dual prospects of Numidian intervention and a substantial bribe, Scipio

now induced the cavalry leader to desert Hasdrubal. It was
the nearest thing to a Roman triumph since the advance on
Carthage, and, in 148, Scipio left for Rome with the Punic
defector to make the most of it.

F

25: *Scipio in Command*

THE chief source for the Third Punic War is Appian, a writer who not only lived much later than the event but whose impression of the world was sufficiently eccentric to place Britain half a day by galley from Spain, and the gulf of Valencia north of the Ebro. Fortunately, Appian's description of the fall of Carthage draws heavily on the lost original by Polybius, an historian of distinction and a witness of the climatic scenes.

Polybius, invaluable to students of Carthage, was a Greek of Megalopolis, in Arcadia. Carried to Rome with a number of suspect Achaeans after the conquest of Macedonia in 168, he formed a close relationship with the victorious Aemilius Paullus and his family, not least the youngest son, Scipio.

Like Thucydides, whose rationalist principles he echoed, Polybius was rare among the ancients for his scientific conception of history, eschewing the legendary traditions of the age. 'In history,' he wrote, 'the end is by real facts and real speeches to instruct and persuade for all time the lovers of knowledge.' He was exceptional, too, for a comprehensive or synoptic view. Thus:

> History is, as it were, an organic whole; the affairs of Italy and Africa are intertwined with those of Asia and Greece, and all have reference to one end.

No man is impartial, and Polybius did not claim to be. Historians, he asserted, should avoid intentionally falsifying facts to favour nations or friends, but they might, he allowed, 'incline the balance.' That Polybius inclined the balance in favour of the Scipionic cause was a small and human price imposed on posterity for the nearest thing it possesses to a clear description of Carthage and her last defence.

The extent to which the Roman family confided in the Greek historian is suggested by a conversation between Polybius and Scipio when the latter was eighteen and burdened with his heritage. 'They consider me unambitious and idle,' complained the youth of his compatriots, 'entirely untypical of a Roman. My family, they say, needs a leader quite the opposite of myself. It distresses me.'

Reassuringly, Polybius promised guidance 'to help you speak and act worthily.' How much Scipio owed to his mentor is uncertain – perhaps less than the teacher liked to think – but there is no doubt that his remarkable progress to high command was accompanied by a real affection for Polybius.

The campaign season of 148 proved depressing for the Romans.

In several ways the Carthaginians were encouraged in their brave defence. With Scipio elsewhere, the sons of Masinissa showed little eagerness to help the invaders; indeed, some Numidian cavalry joined the Carthaginians. While Hasdrubal contrived to get supplies to the city, messengers slipped out to establish ties with distant allies – the Moors beyond Numidia, and the Macedonia pretender Andriscus, then in arms against the Romans. Diplomatic initiatives brought little practical assistance, but helped to keep up morale.

Spirits in the Roman camp were at low ebb. The men had come for easy victory; stayed to get their heads drubbed. The new generals for the year, the consul Calpurnius Piso and his legate Mancinus, appear to have shrunk from asking much of their unhappy troops. Either circumspectly or pusillanimously – perhaps both – the commanders refrained from directing fresh attacks against the city, marching instead on such lesser places still loyal to Carthage as Clupea and Neapolis.

Aimless, desultory, the campaign promised little and, strategically, achieved less. Neapolis, at the base of the Cap Bon peninsula, surrendered, but its merciless sacking by the Romans only stiffened resistance elsewhere. Hippo Acra defended herself so fiercely that the besiegers withdrew empty-handed. It is difficult to see any purpose in the scattered offensive other than a desire for easy booty, a sop to the moody troops. Even then, success was limited.

Dissatisfaction in Rome made way for Scipio. He had returned to Italy to stand for election as aedile; he found himself suddenly within grasp of the consulship. Stories of his martial daring; laudatory letters from soldiers in Africa; the presence of Himilco Phameas in his party – the only glimpse of success so far afforded Rome –, all contributed to a growing conviction that if anyone could bring operations to a speedy conclusion it was Scipio.

When the one objection to his nomination for consul – the fact that he was still six years below the legal age – was discreetly waived, popularity and propaganda did the rest. By direct vote of the people, Scipio was awarded command in Africa not only for 147 but, at least by implication, for as long as necessary to raze Carthage.

Embarking reinforcements, the young general sailed for Africa with a personal friend, Laelius, as his legate, and an entourage reflecting his taste for Greek culture in the persons of his trusted mentor Polybius and the Stoic philosopher Panaetius. It was spring. The red cliffs at Sidi Bou Said stood out vividly from the sea. Carthage, the 'ship at anchor,' lay grandly, defiantly beside her temple-capped citadel.

Scipio returned to the front at a critical moment for the legate Mancinus, who had celebrated the last days of his office with a belated assault on the northern suburbs. Appian, following Polybius, makes this a reckless venture rescued from disaster by Scipio. Other sources, notably Livy, credit Mancinus with some success. At all events, he had run into difficulty and was evacuated from a tricky cliff-top position, perhaps near Cape Gammart.

Recalling the second army of Piso from the country, Scipio set himself to restore discipline to a debased force.

The camp was cleared of all ineffectives, particularly the profiteers who had spawned in large numbers over two years. All superfluous goods were to be sold under supervision by a given date. In a pep-talk to his soldiers, the new commander made it clear that they would be rewarded – but not until victory had been secured.

While Scipio revitalized his army, the Carthaginians took steps to meet a heightened offensive. Of these, the most important was perhaps the transfer of Hasdrubal from Nepheris to assume command of the city's defence. A coarse type of officer, florid, pot-bellied, domineering – in many ways the antithesis of Scipio –, the Punic general was by no means universally popular. He had, however, handled his modest forces with skill against the Romans, and his fire and resolution were formidable.

The Nepheris command now passed to a captain named Diogenes, seemingly a Greek mercenary, while one Bytheas led the cavalry once under Himilco. What proportion of the interior force accompanied Hasdrubal to Carthage is unclear, but 6,000 men were established with the general in a post on the isthmus, close to the triple fortifications.

Hasdrubal's first problem was the sheer expanse of the front. With nothing like the garrison required to man all sectors of the ramparts, his only hope of holding the outer walls of the city was by means of mobile units forewarned of hostile movements. So far, the clumsy assaults of the consuls had allowed the citizens either to mass in advance on the threatened bulwarks, or at least time to limit penetration.

Scipio quickly pointed the need for a new strategy.

In a swift attack on two portions of the wall beside the northern gulf (Sebka er Riana), he succeeded in entering the rural quarter of the Megara with 4,000 troops. That he was forced to withdraw with no more luck than Mancinus had met earlier was due mainly to the density of orchards, olive groves and irrigation channels in the area – features greatly impeding his heavy infantry.

Both sides made new plans. While Hasdrubal withdrew his forward post, Scipio, apprised of the unfavourable nature of the Megara – a gift to light defensive groups –, switched his thoughts to the south, and the precedent of Censorinus. One way or another, the defences of the inner city had to be over-

come. He resolved to take the Byrsa and harbours by direct
assault.

Before he could safely concentrate on this sector, the
isthmus had to be sealed against the influx of supplies to
Carthage, and diversionary movements by her forces. To this
end, the Romans spent the next few weeks on an extraordinary
piece of military engineering : a screen of fortifications covering the entire front of the land wall. These works, found in
part by modern archeologists, were described in detail by
Polybius.

Two parallel trenches were dug from shore to shore across
the isthmus and joined near the water on either side by two
more, completing a quadrilateral. Then the mounds from the
trenches were palisaded – on the section facing Carthage, to a
height of twelve feet. On the same side was built a series of
observation towers, the central of which had a wooden superstructure of four storeys. Loftier even than the nearby city
rampart, this post offered a clear view of the Megara.

The whole undertaking, completed in the face of repeated
Punic sallies, engaged the Roman army day and night for
twenty days. The result was a fortified enclave blocking Carthage from the mainland, defensible by a fraction of Scipio's
total force. Combined with a sea blockade by the Roman
fleet, its effect on the city was grimly claustrophobic. The siege
was now in earnest.

Hasdrubal had pulled into the Byrsa to shorten his defensive
line. The inner walls were strong, the inhabitants resilient.
An inspired leader might have personified the glory of resistance in the crisis, but the stout general, more at home among
his mercenary guards than the citizens, responded with savage
wrath. Dragging his Roman prisoners to the ramparts, he tortured and slew them in full view of their comrades, tossing
the bodies to the ground outside. Those Carthaginians who
protested were also killed.

Hasdrubal's tactics, recalling the horrors of the Mercenary
War, were calculated it seems to commit his men. Perhaps
some of his soldiers had been wavering. But that the mass of

Carthaginians required any such gesture is denied by all the evidence, and a man of sensitivity must have known it so. The crude brutality did nothing for Carthage; plenty for Scipio. His legionaries needed just such a motive for the job ahead.

26: *The 'Final Fifty'*

HAVING garrisoned the fort on the isthmus, Scipio marched the greater part of his army southeast round the city toward the *taenia*, where, like Censorinus before him, he based his fleet. Here, close to the pellucid shallows of the bay of Kram, he was as near as he could get, without breaching the walls, to the vitals of the metropolis.

Immediately to his north lay the flats of the dockland, the rectangular merchant harbour interposing between his viewpoint and the naval pool. The first basin, normally a throbbing pulse of Punic commerce, now languished, its activity confined to the occasional vessel which braved the Roman sea blockade. The second, concealed by its surrounding galley sheds, was of slight concern to Scipio, for Carthage had lacked a navy since Zama. The admiral's tower reared a docile head, its trumpets silent.

Beside the docks stretched the sacred ground of the tophet and the ashes of countless acts of sacrifice, a sanctuary the superstitious Roman troops would hope to by-pass. More appealing to their cupidity were the market between the *cothon* and the near heights, the salubrious buildings round the public square, the neighbouring senate house. Here would be rich loot.

Prominent on the ground rising from the square to the citadel, tall apartment blocks with roof-views of coast and sea would have stood out clearly from the bay of Kram. Among them climbed the narrow roads to the acropolis and to the range of hills – from St Louis northeast to Bordj Djedid – which terminated the northern aspect from the Roman camp. It was amid the wharves, offices, tenements and state buildings of the Byrsa that the struggle for the city would be won and lost.

Beyond the *enceinte*, from easterly Cape Carthage to Cape Gammarth in the north, and throughout the westerly Megara, a scattered population must quickly capitulate once the dense conurbation of the southeast were captured. Trapped between a Roman army in possession of the Byrsa, and Scipio's stranglehold on the isthmus, the people would have lost their one slender life-line with the outer world: the small fleet of merchantmen still defying the sea blockade.

The intrepid captains of this band, homing with the elusive skill that had foiled another generation of Romans in Sicily, delayed the plans of Scipio, whose strategy rested on weakening the city by starvation before mounting his assault. In this policy lay the essential difference between his approach and that of Censorinus, who had attacked an under-armed but robust and spirited populace.

The measure of Scipio's reluctance to take on the Carthaginians, even with his immense force, until they had been enfeebled by lack of food, was demonstrated by the second of his engineering prodigies. Unable to beat the blockade-runners with his navy, he now resolved to build a great mole from the *taenia* across the bay of Kram to the *choma*, or outer quay, shutting off the common entrance to the harbours. For the rest of the summer, the Roman army laboured at the task.

Nearly 800 yards in length (some portions are visible above the water to this day), Scipio's mole was described by Appian as 24 feet wide at the top and 96 feet across the base. At that rate, according to one modern estimate, more than 12,000 cubic metres of stone – possibly as much as 18,000 cubic metres – would have had to be shifted in the construction. Unsurprisingly, the Carthaginians at first regarded the project with scepticism. Then, as the wall progressed and its threat to them became evident, they countered with a scheme of equal magnitude.

This involved two feats: 1, The improvisation of a fighting fleet from old materials; 2, The digging of a new harbour entrance, a direct channel from the naval basin to emerge at

F*

sea north of the outer quay. The second, an enormous operation in which men, women and children all assisted, was the
more remarkable since the Romans, on their own admission,
remained oblivious to the work afoot. Even reports from de-
fecting mercenaries, though describing the incessant sound of
heavy toil, failed to identify its actual source.

Doubtless security precautions were rigorous. Nevertheless,
a characteristic civic responsibility, a closeness amounting
almost to mass stealth, is evidenced. The building of the fleet
was no less secretive. In this, however, the seclusion of the
naval base greatly helped.

Fifty vessels were constructed. Why this had not been done
earlier is unexplained, but probably the armaments drive had
claimed ship-builders for more urgent work. There were other
resource problems. Given a limited supply of materials, should
the Carthaginians create a small navy, outnumbered and out-
weighed by the Roman fleet, or concentrate on vital blockade-
running merchantmen?

Could they, indeed, spare the able-bodied men for a fighting
fleet which, even restricted to fifty ships, might still take a
third or more of Hasdrubal's effectives? Such was the risk, it
seems reasonable to suppose, that it took the dramatic tighten-
ing of the siege under Scipio to give the project impetus.

One thing is certain: had they wished to do so, the Carthaginians had neither time nor the supplies to build heavy-
weight warships. In fact, relatively light, highly manoeuvrable
craft were their preference; skilled seamanship their prime
reliance. Wrote Polybius:

> Their ships were built to move in all directions with great
> agility; their oarsmen were experts . . . if some of their
> vessels were hard-pressed by the enemy, their light weight
> enabled them to withdraw safely and make for open water.
> Should the enemy attempt pursuit, they came quickly about,
> darting round them, attacking on the beam, always haras-
> sing . . .

Experienced handling was important. Punic galleys normally possessed two rudder-oars, one belayed to each side of the vessel. Much of the time only one was used, the other held in reserve. But in battle two helmsmen were employed, operating the rudders simultaneously for maximum manoeuvrability. Without perfect synchronization, the method not only lacked advantage but could prove a grave embarrassment. It followed that practice and teamwork within a fighting crew were vital.

Carthaginian seamen had missed battle experience for many years. Until it got to sea, the new navy could not rehearse old skills – and it could not get to sea until the emergency channel had been finished, for the Roman mole was far across the bay by the time the ships were ready. A special incentive to those labouring on the passage was the fact that the enemy, pre-occupied with his own toils, had left his fleet largely un-attended.

Feverishly, the Carthaginians dug their channel; methodi-cally, the Romans slogged at their pier of stone. Scarcely was the causeway completed, sealing, as its architects believed, the harbour complex, than the citizens broke through the final stretch of land to the north and their fleet appeared at sea. It was a brilliant stroke, utterly surprising the Romans.

But delay in seeking naval action was inevitable. Little value can be placed in the familiar complaint that the Punic mariners wasted time on the open gulf parading their new ships 'in childish but natural glee.' The vessels had never been out of a basin less than 350 yards in diameter – and that with an island in the middle. They took to sea virtually from the building sheds, crews unaccustomed to ships and each other.

The first task of the captains was to get the feel of the vessels, their individual handling qualities, and to allow oars-men and helmsmen time to find rhythm and to rehearse the execution of manoeuvres. It was, in fact, a period not of idle cavorting but of sea trials and integration, with adjustments perhaps required in harbour. Thus, while the case for an im-

mediate attack on the Romans is evident, the Carthaginians
are maligned if their delay is seen as frivolous.

In opting for a couple of days in which to shape for action, the Punic captains were conscious not merely of the
tremendous effort made to float their vessels, but that
these were irreplaceable. The burden on them was a heavy
one.

As it happened, it was too great. Three days after its first
emergence in the gulf, the little navy bravely engaged the
powerful Roman fleet. A brisk but inconclusive battle followed
in which the Carthaginians weathered the odds until evening,
then withdrew toward harbour. The new channel was narrow,
soon congested. Unlike the sheltered and shallow approach by
the bay of Kram, it gave into deep water disposed to a tricky
swell.

While the smaller of the Punic galleys nosed into the
channel first, their larger sisters lay up by the outer quay to the
south, covered by artillery on the city walls and on the quay
itself. The big Roman warships that had followed were baffled.
Attacking head-on, they presented slight targets, but as they
turned to draw off they were broadside to the missile barrage,
highly vulnerable.

The Carthaginians might have been safe had it not been for
a flotilla of five ships from Side in Pamphylia, Asia Minor, on
a mission of goodwill to Scipio. Better seamen than the Romans,
the Pamphylians dropped sea-anchors on long lines and warped
back after running in to strike the Punic ships.

Scipio's captains, grasping the lesson, found themselves able
to inflict heavy damage to the enemy without turning their
prows from his artillery. Night had fallen before the surviving
Carthaginian craft managed to limp into harbour.

Such was the last naval battle of Punic history. Compared
with the great sea struggles against Rome – the victory of the
crows at Heraclea, the Carthaginian triumph at Drepanum,
and other epics – it was an anti-climax, an affair of modest
numbers in which the odds were too uneven to leave the outcome in much doubt. But the challenge of the 'final fifty' was

in the stirring tradition of a people whose seamanship was praised unanimously by contemporaries, not excluding their rivals.

From now on, every citizen would be occupied in land defence.

27: *The Deadly Thrust*

THE day following the naval action, Roman troops equipped with rams and assault machines could have been seen crossing the mole toward the *choma*. Their objective was a defence post on the broad outer quay from which Carthaginian artillery had pounded their warships. Revengefully, the attackers applied their engines to the stronghold, smashing part of its guard-wall.

A vicious struggle ensued for the *choma*, a vital stepping-stone to the docklands. Since the building of the mole, both sides had land connections with the essentially sea-bound quay, whose merits as a missile platform were obvious. The Carthaginians defended it desperately.

In a classic operation against the Roman engines, a party of swimmers from the city scrambled from the water, slipped to the machines under cover of darkness, and suddenly lit torches. Startled by the flaring lights, the Romans responded with a hail of darts. The naked swimmers were vulnerable. With suicidal preoccupation they pursued their task until the siege engines were blazing.

So affected was the Roman camp by the shock of the attack, the fanatical intensity of its participants, that the wisdom of confronting such defenders was widely doubted. Scipio is said to have deployed a cavalry squadron to prevent desertions among his troops. Meanwhile, the Carthaginians repaired the damaged strong-post.

The fight for the *choma* resumed with fresh fury. New attacks were repulsed. Among Scipio's problems was the difficulty of manhandling heavy assault equipment across the slender footway of the mole. Huge metal-capped battering-rams of the type employed by Censorinus would have done the job quickly, but were impractical on the causeway. Such implements demanded the tractive power of men and oxen by the hundred.

Lighter contraptions were brought forward to replace the burnt engines. Still, the Punic post resisted. Only when Scipio, borrowing inspiration from the enemy, resorted to incendiary tactics was he eventually successful. Forcing the defenders from their station with burning projectiles, the Romans occupied the whole outer quay. To prevent its recapture, Scipio built a wall on its landward side behind which he placed ballistae and catapults.

The fall of the *choma*, coming at summer's end, was a death-blow to the harbours. Roman artillery could now cover the merchant pool with heavy missiles (the ancient ballista could throw crushing stones some 400 yards) and cast lighter ones into the naval base. In any case, the impunity with which Scipio's warships were enabled to lie beside the quay denied even the slipperiest of Punic craft use of the new channel.

Carthage entered the winter with starvation not far ahead. Subsistence depended on the gardens of the Megara – a mere supplement, in normal times, to inland and overseas produce – together with some fish and goods smuggled across the lake from Nepheris. Nepheris, still held by the forces of Diogenes, became the next target for Scipio.

Reviving the wilted interest of Gulussa, the Roman commander organized a joint Roman-Numidian campaign against the inland fort. The legate Laelius led the allies, with intermittent supervision from Scipio, who shuttled between his camp and siege headquarters. The operation was opposed more by winter's blows than by the enemy's. Diogenes's mercenaries were in poor heart. The peasant levies enlisted to support them showed less zeal. Most broke and ran at an early stage, to be ridden down and slaughtered by Gulussa's cavalry.

Galled by wintry conditions in their field camp, the legionaries pressed Nepheris, and the promise of shelter, tenaciously. The fall of the stronghold, cutting Carthage's last flimsy lifeline, signalled the capitulation of the few other African towns yet to bow to Rome. Though of little practical assistance, their resistance had helped to keep up spirits in the metropolis.

The most extreme of Punic optimists could no longer dispute the outcome of the conflict. In the course of the winter, the Carthaginians made at least one final attempt to obtain tolerable terms from the Romans. Perhaps it was felt that the approaching termination of the consulship of 147 was a favourable moment. Roman generals were notoriously anxious to conclude their campaigns in time to retire as popular victors. Unfortunately for Carthage, reasoning on these lines was invalidated by confirmation of Scipio's understanding that his command would continue until the war was over.

When Hasdrubal, through the mediation of Gulussa, approached Scipio on behalf of the city, the Roman refused to budge from his purpose of destruction. Though apologists were at pains to stress not only his military competence but his sympathetic qualities, it seems that Scipio lacked the magnanimity, the capacity for the big human gesture, that had made his grandfather by adoption great.

Instead, he displayed mere cunning in offering safe-conduct to Hasdrubal, his family and ten friends of the Carthaginian's choosing. Polybius and the Romans defamed the Punic general, but, whatever his failings, he dismissed the invitation with the contempt it merited. Negotiation impossible, he returned to Carthage for the last scenes of the tragedy.

For three years the city had stood at bay, stripped of empire, bereft of allies, strength ebbing but still dangerous. Even now, her people dying wretchedly of hunger, Carthage evoked fear in her assailants – like some great beast lying mortally crippled with barred fangs. Determined in the spring of 146 to deal the *coup de grâce*, Scipio moved with prudent caution.

The first step was to assure the operation on religious grounds. Omens were consulted to check on the timing; the protective gods of the city entreated 'to forsake the places, temples, sacred sites, the people and the buildings, and depart from them. Cast terror and confusion on the enemy; fly to Rome and her people.' In return, Scipio's chaplains were prepared to promise 'that temples and games shall be founded to honour you.'

This ceremony, the *evocatio*, was followed by the dreadful *devotio*, consigning Carthage and her forces to the demons of the netherworld. Such formulae, vital to troop morale, were essential in the assault of a city whose evil mystique was a watchword in Roman quarters.

Little doubt can have attached to the location of the attack. Throughout winter, Scipio's artillery had commanded the docks from the *choma*. From his camp on the *taenia*, storm-troops could move safely by the mole to the outer quay, a sprint from the merchant harbour. Once this were taken, the section of wall facing the *taenia*, outflanked, would be untenable by the Carthaginians. Roman reinforcements could stream into the city from the southeast.

Accordingly, the assault infantry, under Laelius, massed by the bay of Kram.

Probably supported by amphibious units, the storming party on the *choma* launched the offensive at an early hour. Rising in line from the Roman-built bulwark on the outer quay, the legionaries had the sun behind them, casting bedazzling shafts from their helmets and arms toward the guard posts. Resistance on the seaward side of the harbour was desultory.

Here, cut off in rear by the rectangular basin, the coastal wall was a hazardous station. Hasdrubal seems to have resigned himself to its abandonment, for he promptly set fire to the harbour sheds, covering his tactical withdrawal.

The Roman infantry technique against missile fire, the 'armadillo,' involved a roof of interlocked shields held aloft in formation. In such a fashion the leading units most likely reached the east wall, scrambling on to it with little opposition. According to Plutarch, the foremost troops included the prospective historian Fannius and a youthful brother-in-law of Scipio, Tiberius Gracchus, later of agrarian distinction.

Laelius now found himself amid a bewildering scene of fire and bombardment, partly blinded by swirling smoke. Swiftly turning the confusion to advantage, he picked his way north by the wall to the region of the naval base. This, the Romans quickly overran. Scarcely pausing, the attackers swept boldly against a secondary wall dividing the docks from the city-proper.

Here, the first fierce fighting was encountered. But the rapidity of the Roman advance precluded organized resistance at this point, and Laelius stormed into the narrow, winding streets which characterized the Byrsa.

In such streets the mercenaries of Bomilcar had come to grief at the time of his abortive coup, pelted with missiles from the balconied roofs of the houses. Lacking outer windows, their doors barricaded, the faceless white dwellings were hard to enter. Where the hungry inmates had the strength to bear weapons, they now represented a new peril to Laelius. Circumspectly, he checked the charge, allowing his units to consolidate.

By evening, the Romans had reached the main square and were mopping-up in the rear. Scipio could be pleased with the day's work. The shell of the city had been breached; the docks and surrounding levels cleared. His army had unimpeded access in the southeast, but much yet depended on continued speed. Resistance, so far light, was likely to stiffen if the garrison and citizens of other quarters were given time to concentrate – especially since the heights of the city were still ahead.

Next morning, Scipio called forward fresh troops. Four thousand moved in through the captured walls. They were ebullient. Expectations of easy victory and long-awaited booty had soared overnight. Now, as they advanced among enticing symbols of affluence – rich temples, inviting houses, merchant banks – avarice overcame discipline and they ran amok.

Vital hours were lost in plundering. At one temple, dedicated to the Carthaginian Apollo, shrine and statue were hacked to pieces with swords in the grab for gold. A thousand talents of the stuff were carried off, so the story goes. By the time authority was restored, the day was wasted. Perhaps luckily for Scipio, the richest temple in Carthage, that of Eshmoun, presented an incentive for renewed attack.

It stood a few hundred yards from the square, beyond climbing streets – streets now held in strength by the citizens. None could have forecast the cost of the journey. A week of savage fighting, involving all Scipio's reserves and frightful losses, was to pass before the Romans reached their objective.

28: *The Salted Furrow*

THE total population of Carthage at the start of the siege, including freed slaves, has been estimated at 200,000, of whom about 30,000 bore arms in defence of the city. Some had perished in the fighting over three years; more by starvation. Perhaps 100,000, or thereabouts, occupied the densely urbanized Byrsa in the closing days.

Of these, most must have been enfeebled by hunger, though doubtless Hasdrubal's soldiers were fairly strong. The troops would have secured a priority claim to food. Their vigour could only delay the end. Without ships, or an exit by the isthmus, there was no escape. Either the inhabitants of the tenemented slopes surrendered at discretion, or they died fighting. Temperament dictated the second course.

Three roads led from the square to the vicinity of the temple of Eshmoun, each narrow, lined by multi-storey buildings. Characteristic of such Phoenician cities as Tyre and Motya, where scarcity of space encouraged vertical construction, the tall blocks had become fashionable in the Mediterranean. Occupied by armed men, they were veritable strongholds, every floor a fresh obstacle to assailants; the roofs becoming decks from which missiles could be hurled at troops in the streets below.

Appian recounted the fierce resistance from these tenements: 'The defenders showered projectiles on the Romans from six-storey buildings. Inside, the struggle continued to the roofs, and on planks across the gaps between them. Many people were pitched to the ground, or on to those fighting in the streets.'

The perilous procedure of assaulting rooftops by plank from nearby buildings indicates the difficulty of clearing the tenements from inside. It also suggests the reluctance of the

Romans to take their chances among the plunging bolts and masonry in the streets. Often little more than alleys, the thoroughfares of the Byrsa were not difficult to barricade. Resistance faced the storming troops at every step.

Unnerved by suicidal opposition, by the chilling sights and sounds in the upper town, the legionaries recoiled. Repeatedly, they reformed and charged, to be driven back. Fresh legions were thrown in; exhausted and despondent men pulled out. Squads of Romans were assigned to haul the dead from the streets so that reinforcements would not be obstructed. A day passed; another dawned, and yet another. Through each, the defenders fought with mounting frenzy.

So pressing was Scipio's need for support that he brought his cavalry into the city, a recourse the more exceptional in view of the hilly ground.

According to Appian, the Roman general remained in personal command, without sleep, through the entire attack, snatching refreshment at irregular intervals. Carthaginian fury was matched by Roman savagery. In the buildings, the attackers slaughtered everyone they came across, tossing many of the disarmed to troops below, who impaled them on raised pikes. Dead and dying citizens were used to fill ditches across which advanced Scipio's transport.

'The body of one,' wrote Appian, 'was used to plug a hole.' The brutality, he thought, was 'not deliberate but in the heat of battle,' a distinction lost in the flow of his macabre lines:

> At length Scipio ordered the whole region to be fired and the ruins flattened to make space for his advancing troops. As this was done, the falling buildings included the bodies of many (civilians) who had sought refuge on upper storeys and been burnt to death. Others, wounded and badly burnt, were still alive . . . dead and living were thrown together into pits, and it often happened that those not yet dead were crushed by the cavalry as it passed.

On the sixth day, Scipio, pausing wearily on an 'elevated

place,' surveyed the results of the most protracted and fero-
cious street battle recalled in ancient history. Behind him, the
docks were in ashes. Once-rich temples and monuments had
been torn apart in the scramble for loot. Smoking rubble replaced scores of former dwellings.

Everywhere, bodies festooned the tortured city : young and
old, male and female – dumped uncovered in hollows, sprawled
on footways, protruding amid crumbled masonry and charred
beams.

The Roman losses are not recorded, but they must have been
grievous. Street fighting is costly; against fanatical defenders,
extremely so. Some idea of the carnage may be gained from
the figure given for Carthage's survivors. On the seventh day, a
group of men approached the Romans and offered the surrender of those still in the Byrsa if their lives were spared. Fifty
thousand tragic people emerged – all who remained of garrison
and populace save Hasdrubal and a small band barricaded in
the temple of Eshmoun.

Of this last group, 900 strong, most were men who had deserted from the Roman side during the long siege. They were
excluded from the terms of safe conduct; in no doubt of their
grisly fate if captured.

Carthage was lost.

Withdrawing up the sixty steps to the great shrine, the
doomed guard held first the precincts then, at last, the temple
itself, climbing to the roof with its sweeping view of the blue
gulf. Here, according to the sources available, they perished
like Dido on a pyre of their own firing. Though not improbable, the burning of their refuge suspiciously echoes Scipio's
earlier tactics.

At the last moment, Hasdrubal surrendered his person and
his family.

A dramatic if dubious account of the incident told how the
general's wife appeared briefly from the temple to compliment
Scipio as a noble foe, reviling her husband as a coward and
traitor before consigning herself and their children to the
mounting flames. The story, blatantly Scipionic in bias, flies

THE SALTED FURROW 181

in the face of Hasdrubal's dauntless behaviour throughout the siege. That he declined to perish with Roman deserters could scarcely be held traitorous to Carthage.

Indeed, Scipio himself appears to have regarded his adversary with some respect, for not only was Hasdrubal allowed life and liberty but a peaceful seat of retirement in Italy. Most of the city's other survivors were sold as slaves.

Looting was now officially sanctioned, the rank-and-file permitted to retain the lesser treasures while important items were earmarked for the Roman government. Others were returned diplomatically to Sicily, from which island many works of art had come to Carthage. Acragas regained her prized Bull of Phalaris; Segesta, a valued statue of Diana.

What remained of Carthage was burned, and the empty ruins flattened. Demolition complete, the ceremony of sowing salt in a furrow was enacted to symbolize eternal desolation. Scipio solemnly cursed the site. For ten days, as if loath to abandon its charred womb, a pall of smoke hung over the promontory – the last message from a city which, as Appian put it

had flourished for seven centuries since its foundation, which had ruled vast territories, seas and islands, as replete in arms, fleets, elephants and money as the greatest empires, but had surpassed them in daring and courage, for though disarmed and lacking ships it had withstood siege and famine for three years before meeting destruction . . .

Perhaps sensing the need for a touch of warmth in the victor, the writer added that Scipio 'is said to have wept' when the deed was done. The cause of the weeping is somewhat ambiguous. Seemingly reflecting on the mortality of cities and empires, as of life itself, Scipio turned to Polybius, who was with him, 'and took him by the hand, saying: "This is a glorious moment, Polybius, and yet I am strangely fearful that some day the same fate will befall my own country." '

It was the mark of a great man, in the opinion of Polybius,

to be aware in success of the fickleness of fortune. Apprehension, not remorse, it seems induced the general's tears.

*   *   *

Thus, at a stroke as final in effect as a nuclear missile strike, an entire city, the centre of imperial government – indeed, of a civilization – was blotted from the earth's face. Since Zama, Carthage had languished as a martial power. In some ways she had been archaic, resistant to development; but, in others, virile still and ingenious, commercially adroit and regenerative. Rome built nothing to equal her in Africa for well over a century.

In 122 B.C., the Roman senate proposed to place a colony on the site. The enterprise, dedicated to Juno Caelestis, was doomed from the start by poor omens. It was said that hyenas tore up the boundary marks, recalling Scipio's solemn curse. In 46 B.C., Julius Caesar, pursuing the last of Pompey's supporters to North Africa, camped on the ruins. His decision to rebuild the city for Roman citizens was carried forward by Augustus, and in the pro-consulship of 14 to 13 B.C. the headquarters of the African province was moved there from Utica.

Strabo described the Roman Carthage – *Colonia Julia Carthago* – as among the foremost cities of the empire, but old suspicions persisted in Italy and the colonists were forbidden to replace the walls. After a chequered history of revolt and imperial pretension, during which Carthage became the centre of Christianity in Africa, the city was approached by the Vandals. The belated raising of walls proved a vain expense. Encountering feeble opposition, the Vandals sacked the colony, retaining a mere pirate stronghold there.

In 553 A.D., as *Colonia Justiniana Carthago*, Carthage received 'a last ray of lustre' from the Byzantine general Belisarius who, defeating the Vandals, restored something of the city's former stature. It was shattered, ultimately, by the Arabs. The final devastation, ordered in 698 A.D. by Hasan ibn en-Noman, Gassanid governor of Egypt, left Carthage little more than a quarry from which the passing pageant of North Africa – Berbers, Bedouins, Turks, Spaniards, Italians, Germans, French – built its transient camps.

Of the small band of survivors from Punic Carthage knowledge is minimal. At the beginning of the 1st century B.C., the Roman general Marius, proscribed by Sulla, found scattered groups of Carthaginian origin in the region of the deserted ruins. With pathetic unreality, they sent delegates to Mithridates, king of Pontus, on the Euxine, pledging support for his own fight against Rome.

Few can have escaped assimilation or servitude. It is true that Carthaginian culture lingered in the coastal cities of North Africa, and in Numidia, where the courts encouraged Punic skills, but its erosion was rapid. Customs and religion soon bore Rome's impress. Baal and Tanit (the latter at length identified with Dido) were Romanized by colonial society. The language of Carthage dwindled to dialect, traces of which St Augustine claimed to have recognized in the Libyan tongue for their likeness to Hebrew.

So extraordinary, even in antiquity, did it seem that Carthaginian civilization should have vanished virtually without trace that legend cast her, like Atlantis, as a lost realm, the repository of untold riches lying undisclosed. Nero cherished vain hopes of finding the fabled hoard. Later theorists envisaged the Carthaginians wandering like the tribes of Israel in search of a new home – even settling, improbably enough, in America.

In fact, Carthage's treasures had departed with Scipio. Of racial posterity, there was none. Her genius perished with the city from which it stemmed. For a state once unrivalled as the mercantile hub of the western world, doomsday had arrived 2,091 years before the atom-bomb.

Bibliographical Note

THE list below is intended to give a brief indication of the scope for further reading, not as a catalogue of sources for students. In undertaking a book aimed at general interest, the author has drawn gratefully on the knowledge of a wide range of specialists without whose scholarship any such work would be impossible. In particular, he acknowledges his use as arbiters on the main topics covered as follows: (general) Stéphane Gsell's masterly *Histoire Ancienne de l'Afrique du Nord* (vols i-iv), Paris 1913-29, and the *Cambridge Ancient History*; (Carthage and the western Greeks) Brian Warmington's fine book *Carthage*, London 1969; (the Punic Wars) *Rome Against Carthage*, London 1971, a concise and eminently readable modern study by T. A. Dorey and D. R. Dudley; (the city and its people) *Daily Life in Carthage at the Time of Hannibal*, English trans. London 1961, which upholds the fascination of all works by the great French authority Gilbert Picard, here with C. C. Picard.

ASTIN, A. *Scipio Aemilianus*. Oxford 1967.
CARY, M. & WARMINGTON, E. H. *The Ancient Explorers*. London 1929.
CINTAS, P. *Céramique Punique*. Tunis 1950.
CONTENAU, G. *La Civilisation Phénicienne*. Paris 1926.
DOREY, T. A. & DUDLEY, D. R. *Rome Against Carthage*. London 1971.
DUNBABIN, T. J. *The Western Greeks*. Oxford 1948.
EHRENBERG, V. *Karthago*. Leipzig 1927.
FOUCHER, L. *Hadrumetum*. Paris 1964.
GARCIA Y BELLIDO, A. *Fenicios y Cartagineses en Occidente*. Madrid 1942.

GAVIN DE BEER, Sir. *Hannibal's March*. London 1967.

GAVIN DE BEER, Sir. *Hannibal*. London 1969.

GRIFFITHS, G. *Mercenaries of the Hellenistic World*. Cambridge 1935.

GSELL, S. *Histoire Ancienne de l'Afrique du Nord* (4 vols). Paris 1913-29.

HARDEN, D. B. *The Phoenicians*. London 1962.

HAWKES, J. & WOOLLEY, Sir L. *Prehistory and the Beginnings of Civilization*. London 1965.

JULLIEN, C. A. *Histoire de l'Afrique du Nord*. Paris 1951.

JUNKINS, G. K. & LEWIS, R. B. *Carthaginian Gold and Electrum Coins*. London 1963.

LAPEYRE, G. G. & PELLEGRIN, A. *Carthage Punique*. Paris 1942.

LÉZINE, A. Architecture Punique. Tunis 1961.

MCDONALD, A. H. *Republican Rome*. London 1966.

MOORE, M. *Carthage of the Phoenicians*. London 1905.

MOSCATI, S. *The World of the Phoenicians*. London 1968.

PICARD, G. *Les Religions de l'Afrique Antique*. Paris 1954.

PICARD, G. *Carthage* (trans. Kochan M. & L.). London 1964.

PICARD, G. & C., *Daily Life in Carthage at the Time of Hannibal* (trans. Foster, A. E.). London 1961.

SCULLARD, H. H. *Scipio Africanus in the Second Punic War*. London 1930.

SCULLARD, H. H. *A History of the Roman World 753–146 B.C.* London 1969.

SCULLARD, H. H. *Scipio Africanus, Soldier and Politician*. London 1970.

SMITH, R. B. *Carthage and the Carthaginians*. London 1897.

THIEL, J. *Studies on the Growth of Roman Sea Power in Republican Times*. Amsterdam 1954.

TORR, C. *Ancient Ships*. New York 1964.

TOYNBEE, A. J. *Hannibal's Legacy* (vol i). London 1965.

VOGT, J. (ed.) *Rom und Karthago*. Leipzig 1942.

WALBANK, F. W. *A Historical Commentary on Polybius* (vol i). Oxford 1957.

WARMINGTON, B. H. *Carthage*. London 1969.

WEILL, R. *Phoenicia and Western Asia*. London 1940.

WESTLAKE, H. D. *Timoleon and his Relations with the Tyrants*. Manchester 1952.

WHITAKER, J. I. S. *Motya*. London 1921.